Incredible
ROGERS
PASS

Edited by ART DOWNS

**A CPR rotary snowplow in
a massive avalanche at
Rogers Pass in the early 1900s.**

D0872795

PHOTO CREDITS
B.C. Provincial Archives, 4-5, 13, 21, 22, 26, 30; Canadian Pacific Corporate Archives, 13, 25, 26; Glenbow-Alberta Institute, 15, 16, 17, 19; Parks Canada, 10-11; Tourism B.C., 46, 62, Front Cover; Vancouver Public Library, 28; Ed Cesar, 34, 38, 40, 42; Don Harmon, 57, bottom; Heritage House, 57, top; John G. Woods and Parks Canada, 53, Outside Back Cover.

Canadian Cataloguing in Publication Data
Main entry under title:
Incredible Rogers Pass

ISBN 0-919214-08-8

1, Rogers Pass Region (B.C.) – History. 2. Rogers Pass Region (B.C.) – Description and travel. I. Downs, Art, 1924- II. Series.
FC3845.R615 1980 971.1'43 C84-12780-4
F1089.R615 1980

PRINTING HISTORY
First edition, 1968. Reprinted five times.
Revised edition, 1980. Reprinted 1985.
Updated editions, 1989, 1995.

HERITAGE HOUSE PUBLISHING COMPANY LTD.
Unit #8, 17921 55th Ave., Surrey, B.C., V3S 6C4

Printed in Canada

CONTENTS

**Searching for bodies in the
avalanche at Rogers Pass on March 5, 1910.
Over sixty workmen died. (See page 22.)**

Historical background

by FRANK W. ANDERSON

The mountains of Rogers Pass are
not high measured in terms of Everest
or Annapurna, but they do tower to
over 3,700 m (11,000 ft.) and there are
many of them. They huddle shoulder
to shoulder like the front wall of a
football team and scowl intimidating-
ly at all who approach. Man has
seriously challenged them for only a
century and has more or less had his
way, although the cost has been
several hundred lives.

The first recorded sighting was by
David Thompson of the North West
Company who saw them from a
distance in 1807 as he traversed
Howse Pass to the north. He saw
them again from the Pacific side after
he had followed the Columbia River
round the Big Bend and was descend-
ing to the coast. Caught up in the
hero worship of Trafalgar's great
admiral Horatio Nelson, he named

them Nelson's Mountains. Although Thompson saw them on several occasions afterwards there is no record that he made a serious assault upon them.

In 1813 Alexander Henry, another Company employee, followed Thompson's canoe route. Like his predecessor, he did not make an attempt to cross them. He never made a return trip for the following year he was drowned near Astoria, Washington. In the wake of Thompson and Henry came the fur traders — men who moved with the seasons, were accustomed to hardships, and accepted

nature as they found it. For the next fifty-three years they used the Big Bend — the 304-km (190-mile) detour the Columbia River makes round the northern flank of Nelson's Mountains before dropping south on its journey to the Pacific. The men who came next, however, were less patient. They were the gold-seekers. In 1858 some 30,000 of them stampeded to the Fraser River and gradually moved upstream, fighting fierce rapids and warlike Indians who killed scores of miners before being subdued. The gold seekers filtered into tens of thousands of square miles of wilderness, panning the gravel of innumerable rivers and creeks in search of yellow treasure.

In 1865, four boatloads left Marcus, Washington, to prospect up the Columbia. Establishing a base at "The Eddy" (now part of Revelstoke) they explored the area, striking gold at Carnes Creek some 40 km (25 miles) to the north. Others pushed still farther into Big Bend country, making discoveries on creeks they called French and McCulloch. The steamer *Forty-Nine* was built at Marcus and made numerous trips up the Columbia as far as La Porte, where a rapid barred further progress. But the Big Bend was to prove overrated and its yield of gold so disappointing that miners nicknamed the region "Big Bilk."

While the miners were looking for sudden wealth, other men were interested in the region for a different, more prosaic purpose. On July 8, 1865, the British Columbia government ordered Walter Moberly, civil engineer, to explore the mountains in the vicinity of the Columbia and Kootenay Rivers for passes through which a railway might be constructed to link the western seaboard to the rest of Canada.

Moberly pushed into the region, discovered Eagle Pass through the Monashees and established the possibility of a railway as far as Revelstoke on the Columbia. He explored the old fur trail around the Big Bend and reported that it was a possible route. But realizing that the detour would be costly as well as time-consuming, he turned his attention to the hitherto impassable Selkirks (as Nelson's Mountains were now called, having been renamed in honor of Lord Selkirk after the North West Company and Hudson's Bay Company amalgamated). On September 17, 1865, he started for the frowning mountains.

Moberly and his crew followed the Illecillewaet River eastward some 30 km (18 miles) from its junction with the Columbia at Revelstoke until he came to the Forks. Here a tributary, the North Illecillewaet (now called Tangier), joined the main river. Although the terrain was rugged, Moberly felt it was a feasible route to follow but after exploring the north fork decided that it was impossible as a rail pass and returned to the Forks.

After a brief rest, Moberly announced his intention to ascend the south (or eastern) branch. His decision created consternation among his Indian guides. They warned him of massive snows which leapt from the mountainsides upon the unwary traveller. They spoke of snow so deep that neither man nor beast could move against it. When these warnings failed, they simply sat on their packs and refused to budge. Since the season was well advanced, Moberly temporarily gave up the quest.

In the spring of 1866, he returned to the attack. At the Forks, he split his force into two parties. One he led northward, while the second he dispatched up the south branch of the Illecillewaet under Albert Perry. He

The power of an avalanche such as this one in Rogers Pass is awesome. Trees two feet and thicker are sheared off without pause and railway locomotives lifted from the rails and tossed aside. Over 200 people were killed along the CPR line in Rogers Pass.

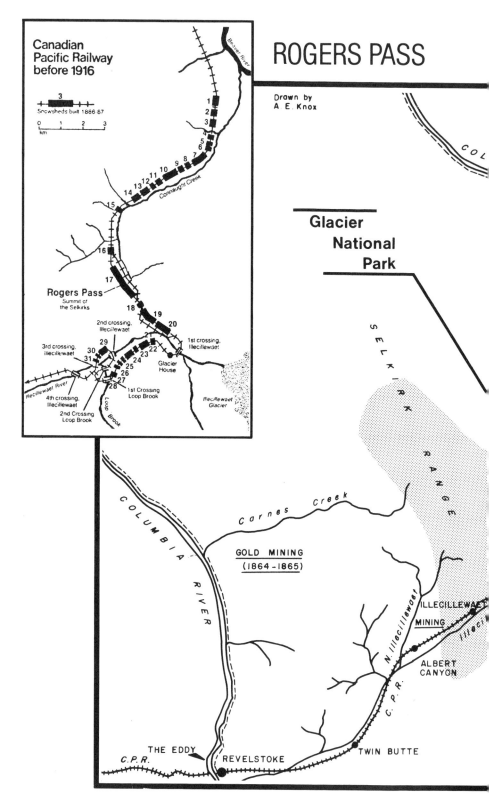

ROGERS PASS

Drawn by
A.E. Knox

Canadian Pacific Railway before 1916

3 Snowsheds built 1886-87

0 1 2 3 km

Beaver River

1 2 3 4 5 6 7 8 9 10 11 12 13 14

Connaught Creek

15

16

Rogers Pass
Summit of the Selkirks

17

18 19 20

2nd crossing, Illecillewaet

1st crossing, Illecillewaet

3rd crossing, Illecillewaet

30 29 31

22 23 24 25 26 27 28

Glacier House

1st Crossing Loop Brook

Illecillewaet River

4th crossing, Illecillewaet

2nd Crossing Loop Brook

Loop Brook

Illecillewaet Glacier

Glacier National Park

COL

SELKIRK RANGE

Carnes Creek

GOLD MINING
(1864-1865)

COLUMBIA RIVER

N. Illecillewaet

ILLECILLEWAET

MINING

Illeci

ALBERT CANYON

C.P.R.

THE EDDY

C.P.R. REVELSTOKE TWIN BUTTE

LEFT: For avalanche protection, in 1886-87 the CPR built thirty-one snowsheds in a 25-km (15-mile) section of the Selkirk Mountains. Today's highway parallels the railway.

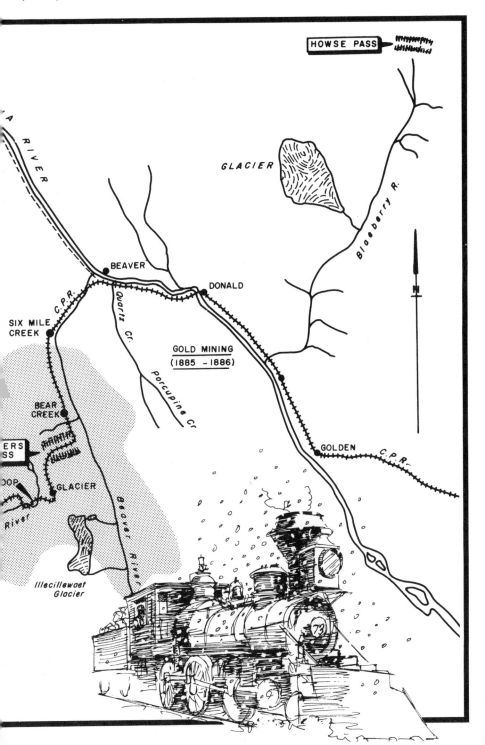

later reported that, while his own efforts were in vain, Albert Perry had followed the south branch sufficiently far to discover that a pass did exist across the Selkirks. However, it is not clear in his report if Perry followed the Illecillewaet far enough to determine where the supposed pass led, but we now know that Perry did not discover a pass.

Before Moberly or others could pursue this promising lead, they were ordered to build roads for the thousands of gold-seekers pouring into the Big Bend country since the difficulties of bringing in supplies through the mountains were enormous. The supply problem was gradually overcome but the miners were defeated by lack of capital. Little gold lay on the surface and few miners had the money to finance extended digging. As a result, all but the most resolute wandered away in search of easier El Dorados and the Big Bend gold rush ended.

When the gold fever had subsided, Moberly was free to resume his attack on the mountains. Unfortunately, interest in the railway had also subsided. He returned to Victoria with the Selkirks only partly conquered.

The formidable peaks and glaciers of the Selkirk Mountains.

In his final report he stated that if a pass existed, it would probably be found along the south branch of the Illecillewaet River.

The huddled Selkirks now had successfully turned back the fur traders, the gold seekers, and the surveyors. The rock barrier was unbroken. But in 1870, the transcontinental railway project was revived. This time the federal government commissioned Moberly to explore the Selkirks around Howse Pass, but scarcely had he begun when in 1872 the government abandoned the route. It had decided to take the line through the Yellowhead Pass to the north.

From 1872 until 1880, the railway project was pursued leisurely by the Canadian government. In 1880, however, the project was taken over by a private company known as "The Syndicate." Promoted by such men as George Stephen, James Hill and Donald A. Smith, the Syndicate brought new vigor to the task of solving the staggering financial and engineering difficulties of a transcontinental railway. Chief among these difficulties was the matter of taking the railroad through the Selkirks. James Hill suggested

Major A. B. Rogers for this job, and pointed to Rogers' credentials. Rogers, born in Massachusetts in 1829, graduated from Yale as a civil and railway engineer. After an apprenticeship on the Erie Canal construction, he tackled the gigantic engineering problem of the Chicago, Milwaukee and St. Paul railroad. His drive, determination and ingenuity promoted him to the forefront of the engineering profession. He came by his title of Major legitimately, having been commissioned during the 1862 Sioux uprising in Minnesota. Rogers was accepted and given the task of finding a route through the scowling Selkirks for Canada's first transcontinental railway, the Canadian Pacific.

Having studied Walter Moberly's reports on the initial exploration of the Selkirks, Rogers decided to attack from the west side. On May 15, 1881, in company with his nephew, Albert L. Rogers and ten Indian packers, he left the Columbia and headed up the Illecillewaet. With supreme confidence, he even arranged a rendezvous for July 1st with a party of his engineers at Exshaw, 48 km (30 miles) east of today's Banff.

Heeding Moberly's suggestion, Rogers ignored the north branch of the Illecillewaet and proceeded up the south branch. Because of the danger of avalanche and treacherous footing, the group travelled early in the morning and after sundown when the snow was frozen enough to bear their weight. On May 28th they reached a second fork in the river. They now knew they were approaching the end of their journey for the river had narrowed to a stream small enough to jump across.

Towards 4 p.m. they skirted a huge mountain, which they appropriately named Syndicate Peak (later Sir Donald) and found themselves at a summit. From here waters flowed east and west. For a better view the party, being "gaunt as greyhounds, with lungs and muscles of the best," ascended a nearby mountain. At one point, four of the Indians fell from the ledge, tumbled down an incline and were lost to view. Said young Rogers: "Our hearts were in our mouths...dead Indians were easily buried, but men with broken legs, to be carried out through such a country and with barely food enough to take us back to the Columbia river on a forced march, made a problem which even strong men dreaded to face." Miraculously, the four escaped injury.

Late in the afternoon, they reached their objective. Crawling out on a ledge, they saw a pass stretching to the northeast. "Such a view! Never to be forgotten!" Albert Rogers wrote. "Our eyesight caromed from one bold peak to another for miles in all directions. The wind blew fiercely across the ridge and scuddy clouds were whirled in the eddies behind the great towering peaks of bare rock. Everything was covered with a shroud of white, giving the whole landscape the appearance of snow-clad desolation."

A pass through the rock barrier had been found.

The following year, tackling the Selkirks from the eastern side, Major Rogers left with a party of five on July 17th. They followed the Beaver River into the mountains and by July 24th found themselves standing at the source of the Illecillewaet River. Rogers returned to base camp, secure in the knowledge that the Selkirks could be conquered.

"The work in the Selkirks will be very heavy and expensive," he reported to CPR general manager Van Horne on January 10, 1883, "but I

A CPR passenger train in the early 1890s at Rogers Pass Station with Mount McDonald towering over 3,000 m (9,000 ft.). On January 30, 1899, an avalanche demolished the station and the roundhouse at lower left, killing ten people.
Below: A construction crew at work on a snowshed in Rogers Pass in 1886.

believe that the increased cost will be fully justified by great saving in distance and the cost of operation."

Building the Railway

Following Major Rogers' history-making treks to the summit of the Selkirks and his favorable report, teams of surveyors and wagon road builders swarmed through Kicking Horse Pass and headed for the Columbia River to a tent community given the optimistic name Golden City. Next came those who built the roadbed for the tracks, hewing and hacking at the forest, dynamiting stubborn knobs of rock, gouging at the dirt with horsedrawn scrapers. They moved slowly, by-passing or leaping streams and gorges, pushing westward foot by hard-won foot. Then came the bridge builders, filling in the gaps. They were followed by the track-layers — marching along with twenty men to a rail, singing, dancing and carousing their way across the plains and into the foothills. By the end of December 1883, the tracks lay covered in snow at Bow Valley Summit in the Rockies.

The next year was a hectic one for the railroad builders as they pushed through the formidable Rockies to the even more formidable Selkirks. The CPR advertised for 4,000 men with pay $2 a day and another 50 cents for overtime. In early April 1884 the camps began to stir. The surveyors peered deeper into the mountains; the supply road (or tote road) builders pushed towards Golden City on the Columbia, and the track-layers forsook the pleasures of Silver City (near Calgary) for the hard grind ahead.

Silver City had started out as an ambitious little mining camp in the early 1880s, but never amounted to anything until the track-layers arrived. Almost overnight it swelled to a bulging 4,000 with most of this population seeming to bulge out of the numerous saloons. With the departure of the railroad builders, Silver City shrank to its normal 351.

Construction across the open prairie presented few problems. On May 27, 1884, the last spike in the Northwest Territories — now Alberta — was driven by Mrs. F. P. Brothers, wife of the superintendent, at the Great Divide where water flowed east to Hudson Bay and west to the Pacific Ocean. The first spike in British Columbia was driven by Mr. Dickie, a government railway inspector. Scarcely anybody but the participants of the little ceremony in the Rockies was impressed.

There had been few casualties during construction westward from St. Boniface into the foothills, but on August 2, 1884, the first major accident occurred. At the point called second crossing of the Kicking Horse River, Engine No. 146 went out of control coming down a grade. To meet such emergencies spur lines had been constructed up the mountainsides at steep angles to slow down runaway trains. An alert trackman, seeing the careening train, threw the switch and detoured the runaway onto a safety line. Unfortunately, the engineer forgot to apply his brakes after hitting the spur line and the train roared up the incline and smashed into an enormous rock at the end. There were some seventy Swedish workmen on the train, and many panicked and jumped from the moving train onto the rocks. One man was instantly killed, while an unknown number died from injuries. Fearful of frightening off new labor, construction bosses tried to keep secret such accidents.

Mountain fever also claimed many workers, but no accurate record remains of its victims. During cold, damp weather, the fever was at its worst and many a gandy-dancer succumbed and was buried quickly and quietly. Here and there a man was killed by falling rock or some other misadventure. In early October, for instance, a young Swede was killed at Maloney's camp, just outside of Golden City, when some dynamite exploded accidentally. Ten others in his crew were injured. Nevertheless, considering the dangers involved and the number of men engaged, the project had thus far not been too costly in human lives. But construction crews were approaching Rogers Pass — and the shoulder-to-shoulder Selkirks were not to surrender gracefully.

As the CPR pushed westward into the mountains, it made and then unmade several railside communities. Among those destined to survive was Golden City. Early in 1884 it was a sleepy tent town with one main street on which Dick Sanderson operated the CPR hotel. Then in August rails arrived and the settlement was for a time the end of steel. With whiskey at 50 cents a

Construction crews at Golden in 1884 and, top, the community about 1888.

15

glass and construction crews lonely and thirsty, there was potential for trouble. But a detachment of North West Mounted Police under Inspector Samuel Steele took up winter quarters in tents by the tracks and maintained order. Then as abruptly as they arrived the construction crews vanished northward to the first crossing of the Columbia River on the way to Rogers Pass.

Here a community which became known as Columbia Crossing, then Donald, sprang to life in October 1884. It was reported to have "more saloons and restaurants than houses of any other line of business." A roving reporter for the Calgary *Herald* described the town as a "dirty, noisy, profane, reckless western town."

Whiskey was brought in from the U.S. and from Kamloops by pack trains. It retailed at $15 to $20 a gallon, finding outlets in Bob Philips' saloon, the Cosmopolitan, the Queen of the West, and the Italian and French quarter saloons. The Italian Saloon was a little hut 12 x 16, where the barkeep was a woman — "but what a woman!" The social life consisted of drinking, gambling and dancing. Music was an integral part of the camp and the main instruments were the fiddle and accordion. Nina Dow, Nellie and Ellen Swift, Emma Stewart, Maud Lewis, Agnes Morris and Nellie Goodrich were the prominent call-girls of the day, popularly referred to as "fallen angels."

The favorite gambling games were Seven-Up and Stud Poker. It was in Bob Phillips' saloon on the night of November 22, 1884, that Tom Evans drew his revolver and took a pot shot at Phillips, but missed his man and struck George Hide — who was standing behind the intended victim — inflicting a severe wound near the right eye. Evans held off the astonished patrons with his revolver and escaped. Despite a determined search by the police, he was never brought to justice.

There was a constant battle between the whiskey runners and the police. Hampered by a law which restricted their activities to within twenty miles of the right-of-way, the police could do little but search incoming trains and watch for the approach of the illicit packers. Another daily

function was to round up the more obvious drunks. On October 30th, for example, the police escorted fifteen celebrants to Golden for the usual fine and warning.

Farther into the mountains 22.5 km (14 miles) from Columbia Crossing, Beaver Creek sprang up when winter stopped construction. Since Swedes formed nearly two-thirds of the population, favorite gathering places were the large number of Swedish restaurants. Saloons, however, were equally popular. One report noted that while there were only four stores, there were ten times that many watering places. That winter a bootlegger named McCallum introduced a new drink. To help him in his illicit smuggling of liquor, he constructed a can with an inner compartment. The inner compartment contained coal oil; the other, alcohol. When the Mounted Police wanted coal oil — they got it; and when the citizen wanted something to light his own inner lamp, he got that. A plug between the two compartments was so contrived that in the event of a raid the two liquids could be combined into something that tasted like whiskey but burned poorly in a lamp.

Despite the large number of rough and ready characters, there was little lawlessness. Nevertheless, two killings occurred. The first was on September 20, 1884, when a camp barber from California attempted to eviscerate James Finn, a construction foreman. He succeeded only in slicing Finn's clothing, who then drew a revolver and shot the barber dead. Finn was later arrested by Inspector Steele's NWMP and brought to trial. He pleaded self defence and was acquitted.

Later in the year, a murder took place outside Golden City. On December 4th a prospector named Baird set out with two companions for Calgary. It was no secret that he had enjoyed a good year in the mountains. Riding single file, the little party proceeded eastward to a point near Johnson's ranch, some 22.5 km (14 miles) from Golden. Suddenly a shot knocked Baird from the saddle. The other two men fled, but not before the unseen sniper had wounded one severely in the leg. When the rescue party reached the scene, they found Baird dead and $4,500 in gold dust missing

At left is Donald in the winter of 1884-85, a single street of log buildings. Above is Beavermouth — also known as Beaver Creek, Beaver River and The Beaver — in 1884-85. The men are lined up outside the Queen of the West Hotel.

from his saddle bags. No one was ever apprehended for the murder.

A humorous incident arose out of the tragic affair when a man named McIntosh, who owed considerable money, took advantage of the situation and circulated the news of his own murder. Stone-hearted creditors, failing to be duped by his obituary, tracked him down the following spring to a construction camp in Rogers Pass.

The year 1884 closed on a tragic note. On New Year's Eve, Constables Percival and Ross, tired of waiting for a train ride from Golden City to their detachment at Third Siding, decided to walk. Both men were inadequately clad and wore light, low shoes. At 2:30, Constable Percival arrived at Third Siding, almost frozen and exhausted. Back-tracking on the trail, the search party located young Ross lying beside the track. Percival, risking his own life, had covered him with his coat. His lungs, feet and hands frozen, Constable Ross died that night at the barracks.

Although the end of track remained at Beaver Creek during the winter of 1884-85, the tote road which carried supplies had been completed to Farwell, today's Revelstoke. From the tote route, engineers kept a close watch on the snow in Rogers Pass.

On February 8, 1885, there were three gigantic snow slides. At McKenzie Camp, 9.5 km (6 miles) west of the summit, a man named Robert Miller was caught and buried by an avalanche. Two miles away, at McDermot's Camp, a slide buried three men who were never found. The third slide was at the summit where a man named Hill had built a store. Fortunately, only the skirt of the slide struck the store and the men inside were able to scramble out through the windows.

Although an attempt was made to minimize the danger from slides and news of deaths suppressed, workmen began to leave for the east, fearing the dangers ahead. Their apprehension would prove well founded.

Towards the end of February, a second slide wiped Hill's store off the map. A short distance away another hurtling mass of snow and ice swept away over $65,000 worth of contract supplies. Salvage work minimized the loss to $10,000 worth of equipment, but six men were known to have perished. It was generally believed that many others had perished in the disastrous February slides and their deaths concealed.

Despite these early proofs of danger, almost 7,000 men were recruited in the spring and at the end of March camps broke winter quarters and began pushing the rails through Rogers Pass. Despite the early start, work stopped in a few days when workers went on strike and only a firm stand by Steele and the eight other NWMP under him when faced by a mob of 700 men prevented a riot. Harold Fryer, author of several books in the Frontier series, wrote of the incident:

"After Christmas 1884, Steele moved his headquarters from Golden to Beaver River, then a mile from the end of the rails. In the area were located about as unsavory a bunch of hooligans as could be found anywhere. They had set up bars and were preying on the construction workers by rolling any who got drunk on their rot-gut booze. Because the railway's manager of construction, James Ross, wouldn't allow his trains to bring in food to this rough segment, they generally got their supplies by stealing them. Consequently, the police had their hands full. Then as if there wasn't already enough trouble, the railroad workers went on strike.

"All through February and March 1885 dozens of workers complained to Steele that their pay was being held up and that they would strike if it didn't soon come through. Steele tried to persuade them to be patient. 'Your pay is guaranteed by the Canadian government,' he told them. It did no good. The workers were agitated by rowdies who had worked on the Northern Pacific in the U.S. and on April 1 they walked off the job.

"Steele expected trouble from the workers and it wasn't long in coming. A couple of days after the strike began Sergeant Fury and three constables had to hold off a large group of armed men who were trying to stop a train load of tracklayers from working. Fortunately the Mounties met the mob, who were firing revolvers and creating a great uproar, at the mouth of the narrow Beaver River Canyon and were able to stand them off without anyone getting hurt. When the strikers saw that Fury's men weren't backing off, they decided to call it a day and let the tracklayers go back to work.

"During this time Steele had been incapacitated with a severe case of flu. And while Fury was engaging the strikers at the canyon, Constable Kerr had gone to the end of the track for a bottle of medicine for his boss. On his way back he heard one of the troublemakers trying to incite a group of strikers to attack the Mounted Police barracks. He immediately tried to arrest him but got a severe pummelling and was forced to leave without his intended prisoner. A few minutes later Kerr met Sergeant Fury who brought

North West Mounted Policeman Sam Steele, foreground, and his detachment in 1885. The man at left is Sergeant Bill Fury.

the news to Steele. 'It's a pity he attempted the arrest without enough help,' said an unhappy Steele. 'But what is done is done. Now we've got to take that man at all costs — we can't let the rest of the gang think they can play with us. Take what ever men you need, Fury, and bring that man in.'

"Off went Fury only to return a short time later with a torn jacket. 'The gang took the prisoner away from us,' he told Steele.

" 'That's too bad,' replied Sam a little sarcastically. 'Now take your revolvers and shoot anyone who tries to interfere with the arrest!'

"Fury was off again, this time taking with him Constables Fane, Craig and Walters. A few minutes later a shot rang out and George Hope Johnston, a Federally appointed magistrate who acted as Steele's deputy, solemnly intoned, 'There's one of them gone to hell, Steele!'

"The two men stepped to the office window to see Constables Craig and Walters dragging a man across the bridge that separated the barracks from the shanty town of Beaver River. The prisoner was kicking and cursing, ably abetted by a woman dressed in red, who was shrieking and calling the policemen some very uncomplimentary names. Though still terribly weak from his illness, Steele grabbed a rifle and ran out to aid Fury and Fane, who were trying to keep the mob from crossing the bridge.

" 'Arrest that woman and bring her along!' he shouted to Fane, and to the menacing mob he gave a stern warning. 'Hold it right there or we'll open fire!'

"The mob answered with jeers and curses. 'Look at the bastard,' said one. 'His own death bed makes no difference to him.'

"Sam may have looked as though he wasn't long for the world, but his stance indicated plainly that if he was to depart, he would be taking a few strikers with him. While he and his men covered the mob, Mr. Johnston read the Riot Act. Steele again told them to move off or he and his men would open fire. By this time quite a number of well-armed town citizens had gathered to back up the police. It was all that was needed — the riot was over.

"It turned out that the man Johnston thought had been sent to Hades was only wounded by Sergeant Fury. He was treated by CPR doctors, fined $100 by Magistrate Johnston and turned loose. Other strikers who were arrested received the same light treatment. It was all that was necessary for on April 7 the workers got their pay and the strike ended."

With the men back on the job, the task of breaching the barrier of Rogers Pass continued. The original survey had proposed to carry the railway high along the side of Syndicate Mountain (now Sir Donald), but the avalanches convinced Major Rogers that this was impractical and dangerous. A safer route would be lower down the mountain, but a lower route along the mountainside meant that the rails had to drop 150 meters (500 ft.) in so short a distance that the railway grade would be too steep. The problem was solved by manager of construction James Ross.

He designed a double loop along the base of three mountains. The loops added nearly 5 km (3 miles) to the length of the section, but enabled rails to be laid along the valley clear of the most formidable slide areas. When completed the rails descended from the summit to Ross Peak in two circles. Most of the span was carried on wooden trestles, one over a mile long. The bottom of the loop ended in the valley of the Illecillewaet River whence it descended to Revelstoke and through Eagle Pass to Kamloops.

In the heart of the Selkirks, the builders realized that at best they could only afford protection against the avalanches of snow and ice that swept down the slopes. Over 6.4 km (4 miles) of snowsheds were completed in 1885-86, and each year after that there was a constant battle with the elements in the Pass. With an eye on the tourist trade, the CPR laid two sets of tracks at the summit. The winter tracks led through an enormous snowshed, while the summer tracks were laid in the open so that travellers could enjoy the magnificent view.

With the summit and the loop conquered, construction of the rest of the line through the Pass was relatively easy, although it involved several crossings of the Illecillewaet River. Finally, on November 7, 1885, the east-bound tracks joined the west-bound at Craigellachie, B.C., and the last spike was driven by Lord Strathcona, a financial partner in the railway. The historic spike was not gold but an ordinary iron one. CPR president Cornelius Van Horne did not like unnecessary expenses or long speeches. His address to those at the ceremony consisted of fifteen words: "All I can say is that the work has been well done in every way."

On June 28, 1886, the first transcontinental train left Montreal for the west coast, thundered through the Rogers Pass with the help of a pusher on July 2nd, and puffed into Port Moody just outside of Vancouver on July 4th. Twenty-one years after Walter Moberly made his first explorations

Rogers Pass village in 1886. At left is the Woodbine Hotel, complete with a false front which hides the rough log construction and primitive inside facilities.

toward Rogers Pass in an attempt to find a route for a railway, Canada had finally been linked by twin steel rails.

The White Executioner

On April 21, 1886, the CPR began opening the road through Rogers Pass after the winter shutdown. Snow plows and crews of men spread out along the line, preparing it for regular traffic. It was the first move in a long struggle during which men gambled their lives against the vagaries of nature.

The first victim was Thomas Williams, locomotive foreman at Donald. On July 8, 1886, Williams slipped on a grease spot and fell into the path of an on-coming train. He was killed instantly. In December 1887, cyclonic winds picked a man up and "whirled and twisted him so rapidly and spirally that when dropped he was a limp mass without a bruise or break in skin or clothing yet with all his bones broken or dislocated."

In the next seventy-five years, over 260 men lost their lives, most by avalanches. The first major disaster occurred at old Rogers Pass Station.

On January 30, 1899, an enormous avalanche broke loose just after 3 p.m. and plunged towards the little town. Station master Albert Cator was talking to a young man at the station door. When they heard the slide coming, they rushed onto the platform. Just then the slide struck the building. Cator was swept away, but the young man dropped to the ground and was buried up to his neck. Miraculously, he survived. Not so fortunate were Mrs. Cator and her two children. They perished in the ruins of the station. Annie Berger, a waitress, survived with a broken leg. The night telegraph operator was asleep in the bunkhouse when the slide struck. Rescuers found him in his bed, suffocated. Frank Vago, who coaled the locomotives, was in the bunkhouse. He was picked up and jammed between the joists, upside down, but somehow survived.

On the tracks, section foreman Ridley was working inside a boxcar, with a helper on top. The helper saw the slide coming, hollered a warning and jumped. He landed inches clear of the skirt of the avalanche, but Ridley was swept away by the churning mass of ice and snow. Two workmen in the

Rotary snowplow and crew clearing a path through an avalanche in the early 1900s.

nearby roundhouse died, while two companions were brought out alive. In all, eight persons perished. It was an ominous preview of worse disasters.

The same day, a second slide broke through a snowshed near the summit, killing an Italian workman inside. The following day, as a snowplow strove to clear the shed, its rotary blade critically injured three Italian workmen, one of whom died later.

One of the first men on the scene of the accident was George Williamson who brought in the medical supply train. Williamson, who started as a wiper at Donald in September 1892 and later became an engineer on trains in Rogers Pass, knew well the constant hazards from slides. Typical was one in the spring of 1906.

"We were widening out what had been a slide," he recalled. "I was coupled onto the rotary, pulling out timber from the slide. I saw some of the boys begin to run. My engine and the rotary were just outside the snow shed and when I saw them starting to run, I knew there was a slide coming and I started to back up. I got the engine inside the shed when...Bingo!...away goes the rotary. The engineer of the rotary, Jim Campbell, and his fireman had jumped and were hanging onto my pilot as I back in. Knocked the rotary away — oh say — 75 to 100 feet. Smashed it all to pieces. It broke off my push casting. There must have been eight, ten, twelve men buried.

"When we dug out the men on the extra gang, I said to Tom Wilson, the foreman, 'Tom, do you think you got all the men out!' So he counted them.

" 'By golly, George,' he said, 'There's one missing!'

"Well, they dug around in the snow and they touched this fellow and dug him out. He was unconscious, but he lived."

Although the tunnels and snowsheds were a necessary precaution in the mountains, they were also a hazard. Water dripping from the ceilings froze on the rails, frequently stalling trains. At Laurie tunnel, the Company constructed large wooden doors at one end in the hope of eliminating drafts which froze the water deep in the tunnel. Said an old-time railroad man: "I went up there as a young buck, firing, and there was many a time we'd slip to a standstill and I've got down and put my face to some water in Laurie tunnel to get air. There was so much gas, and no draft to take the smoke away. But you'd always have to be careful when you came to the end of the tunnel for fear the watchman wouldn't have those damned doors open."

Some winters in Rogers Pass were comparatively peaceful, but not 1910. Massive snowfalls were followed by frost and thaw — ideal avalanche weather. There were numerous slides in late January and all through February, and the rotary plow crews and the extra gangs of Japanese and Italian laborers became accustomed to being called out in the middle of the night to attack a new slide. The frequent deluges of snow continued into early March, causing a massive slide March 2nd which held up passenger trains at Revelstoke and Calgary. By March 4th, the line was reported clear.

Passenger train No. 97, the most celebrated train on the western run since it had been held up twice by robbers, (see Heritage House book *Bill Miner....STAGECOACH & TRAIN ROBBER)* left Donald, where it had been waiting for the signal that the tracks were clear, and moved into Rogers Pass. Shortly after it had passed through Bear Creek, a slide took place, and No. 97 was moved to Rogers Pass Station for safety.

W. C. Waddel of New York was a passenger and noted: "We were six hours late leaving Winnipeg, and three hours late leaving Calgary. To this circumstance we may probably owe our lives. Friday afternoon, just as the train was nearing Bear Creek Station, there was a succession of slides on the adjacent peaks, but not near enough to endanger the railway line. A brakeman was sent back to flag another train in the rear. A few minutes later (some say as little as four minutes) we heard a mighty roaring sound as a slide crashed onto the rails around the bend 200 yards away behind us. The brakeman hurried back covered with snow. He had run for his life when he heard the slide approaching. As it was, he just escaped by a miracle as he was covered with snow from head to foot. He missed the mighty avalanche by only a few feet.

"At Bear Creek Station we were not out of the danger zone as the mountains there rise precipitously. Just as darkness was approaching, we got word of the first slide...."

The first slide had come down opposite Shed No. 17, burying the tracks up to 6 meters (20 ft.) deep. Immediately a crew was sent to the scene. A rotary plow pushed by a locomotive and accompanied by three gangs of laborers and a bridge gang started clearing the main line. The rotary blew away the bulk of the snow, then the Italian and Japanese crews moved in with pick and shovel to clear the tracks.

A few moments before 11:30 that night while the crews were busy clearing the last remnants of the slide, Bill Lachance, fireman on the rotary plow, climbed down from his engine and strolled over the bridge to the north side of Bear Creek. Scarcely had he reached the north bank when a terrible wind rushed down the mountainside — the first warning of a slide. Picked up by the wind, Lachance was whisked through the air and flung into the brush. Behind the wind a massive wedge of snow hurtled down and engulfed the train and workers. Then a deadly calm settled over the scene.

At the first report of the accident a relief train consisting of some 200 men, nurses and doctors was dispatched from Revelstoke, 72 km (45 miles) to the west. The telegraph lines were down across the slide and it was difficult to get an accurate picture. But as word was brought back by messenger from the dreadful scene a mile west of Rogers Pass, the full magnitude of the disaster of that March 4th night became evident. Hurtling down from the slope, the slide had engulfed a quarter mile of track and dropped 450 meters (1,500 ft.) into Bear Creek chasm. Over sixty men had vanished.

Unable to use a rotary plow for fear of cutting the bodies in the slide, the CPR called upon men from nearby logging and mining camps to assist. At one time, over 600 men with picks and shovels were digging through the snow, in places piled nearly 9 meters (30 ft.) deep. Some men were found in the hard-packed snow with their own picks and shovels in hand. Two Japanese workers were dug out, clasped in each other's arms. Another Japanese trackman was found with a knife in one hand and a plug of tobacco in the other.

C. G. Anderson, a commercial traveller from Toronto, was among those on Train No. 97. Anderson gave the following account: "Picture an area 20 miles square, with Rogers Pass as the center of this area covered by millions of tons of snow, half ice, and here close to Rogers Station great trees and boulders torn up and hurled down from the mountain sides into this canyon (Bear Creek) upon the work train and the laborers without a moment's warning. I shall never forget the scene as I went down from our train to see them digging out the bodies of the unfortunate men. While there seeing the brave fellows who were taking their lives in their hands at this work — for so great was the danger of another slide that the passengers were warned against going to the scene — I saw the bodies of three white men and several Japanese taken out cold and stiff in death.... Not a bruise was to be found on any of the bodies that I saw taken out. Like white and bronze statues, the whites and Orientals were recovered one by one.

"It was a tragic spectacle that we witnessed. The rotary engine weighing over 100 tons, as well as a number of cars, had been actually lifted from the main line and hurled in the air onto the top of the roof of the snowshed 40 feet above. The engine lay upside down, a mass of wreckage, and twisted out of all semblance to its original shape. The cars were shattered into splinters. Underneath the engine, several bodies were found. Nearly all the railway men were buried under tons of debris ... the hands of nearly all the victims were extended in front of their faces as though they had been animated with the idea of self-preservation in the fatal moment when the avalanche descended. The faces nearly all wore a peaceful look.

"As victim after victim was recovered, the bodies were strapped onto

Interior of a Rogers Pass snowshed in 1889.

improvised toboggans and hauled to Glacier Station, three miles down the slope."

Another eyewitness account was provided by Joe Godfrey who helped in rescue efforts. A member of a bridge crew, he spent fifty years in the CPR's mountain division before retiring. He recalled that most of those dug up were standing. "We found three foremen," he said, "standing facing one another as if they'd been chatting. One even had his pipe in his hand. Another fellow, a Japanese, had his left leg bent, still standing up, as if he'd taken the first step to climb out. Another man we found still had a cigarette paper between his fingers. He was just about to roll a smoke."

Since officials feared that many of the men had been carried by the slide into the deep gorge of Bear Creek, it was almost impossible to count the number of victims. They began a canvas of all the section house quarters in the vicinity. The two engineers, W. Phillips and A. Potruff, were known missing. Fireman A. Griffith from the locomotive was also missing. Conductor R. J. Buckley and roadmaster J. D. Fraser were gone and presumed dead. The survey of the section gangs revealed that foreman Albert Johnson, Chuck Anderson and E. Wellander and all their crews had been killed.

D. J. McDonald, bridge foreman for the area, was found in the slide. An exceptionally heavy and powerful man, McDonald had evidently been covered with almost five feet of snow, but had retained sufficient consciousness to begin to struggle out by pushing the snow under his feet and working upward. When found, he had moved two feet and had only another three to go to reach the air.

When the final tally was completed, it was found that sixty-two men had perished in the catastrophe. Only Bill Lachance survived.

The Railway Retreats
While 1910 was a bad year for slides, 1911 and 1912 were worse. Nearly 100 slides came down, making railroading through the narrow pass a hazardous and costly business. The bulk of the damage was being done in the area of the Loop, the 8-km (5-mile) stretch which comprised the geographical structure known as Rogers Pass. In places, even a small slide tied up the line for hours. The nature of the snow in this region was another concern. In most instances, the snow froze almost instantly it settled, forming a hard shell over the ties and rails. The long Loop with its 6.4 km (4 miles) of snowsheds and trestles was particularly vulnerable in winter.

Finally, the CPR prepared to beat a strategic retreat. Orders were issued to proceed with the construction of a tunnel through Mount MacDonald to eliminate Rogers Pass. In 1913 CPR engineers began to drive a small, pioneer tunnel into the heart of the mountain. At top speed, they pushed the pioneer tunnel ahead and in one thirty-day period drove 245 meters (817 ft.) into the rock. From the pioneer tunnel — the first American tunnel system in which this technique was tried — the engineers worked outward towards the limits of the final tunnel which was to be 23 by 29 ft. and which would accommodate a double set of tracks, carved through almost 8 km (5 miles) of solid rock.

Then World War One began in 1914 and reports of the tunnel's progress were replaced by more important news from Europe. But deep in the heart of Mount MacDonald, the work continued. Without fanfare, the Connaught Tunnel went into operation in 1916. Eight kilometers (5 miles) in length, it eliminated over 2,300 degrees of curvature in the original track, cut out nearly 8 km (5 miles) of snowsheds, and reduced the summit by 162 meters (540 ft.). The cost was nearly $10 million, of which $2.5 million was for dynamite.

With the completion of the tunnel, several changes took place in the pass. A world-renowned CPR hostelry, Glacier House, began to fall into disuse and the town of Rogers Pass, survivor of nearly thirty years of battle with the slides of March, passed away. Because the new tunnel enabled trains to move faster and because improved equipment was being sent into the mountain region, divisional headquarters was moved from Donald to Golden, and Donald disappeared.

Rogers Pass, having turned back the fur traders and the miners, had bested the railroad builders. True, the Selkirks had been conquered, but Rogers Pass itself, that beautiful, dangerous stretch of natural perfidy, had won again. Although the worst section had been bypassed, there was to be one more major tragedy.

The late days of February 1936 brought frost and thaw and winds, and experienced railroad men girded for another battle with nature. Late in the evening February 29, rain began to fall on the mountain slopes around Albert Canyon, eating into the piled up snow. Avalanches plummeted down the mountainsides, blocking the tracks between the west end of Connaught Tunnel and Revelstoke. The rain continued through March 1st.

Engineer Percy Shafer, hauling a load of livestock from Calgary to Vancouver, passed through Connaught Tunnel about 1 a.m., March 2nd. As he started down the grade towards Revelstoke, he ran into a slide some 30 meters (100 ft.) long just west of Illecillewaet Station. The engine was derailed and remained in the fast-freezing snow bank.

An auxiliary outfit clearing tracks nearby was immediately summoned to help in righting the engine and clearing the line. Two section crews, comprising fourteen men, were picked up at Illecillewaet and brought to the scene.

The rain continued.

Unable to get at the stricken engine, the crew decided to uncouple the train of bawling livestock and pull it back to Illecillewaet. This was done, but when the section crew returned to the scene, they discovered that the locomotive tender still blocked their approach to the engine. Uncoupling the tender, they hooked a cable over the drawbar of the tender, pulled it free and began to haul it up the slope towards Illecillewaet. Ernest Jones, a trainman, B.C. Calder, conductor of the wrecker crew, and Andrew Sheppherd, a car repairman, climbed aboard the tender for the ride back to town. It was then almost 2:30 a.m.

As soon as the tender was pulled free, the track repairmen crawled down the cut behind the stalled locomotive and began to replace a track which had been torn loose and to remove the frozen snow around the engine itself. Five men — engineer Percy Shafer, telegraph operator John R. Roland, mechanics Dick Cossar and G. B. Alexander, and trainman Hans

Haug — gathered in the cab of the derailed locomotive for protection against the wind-driven rains and the chill of the night.

Proceeding cautiously because of the extreme slide danger, the wrecker backed uphill towards Illecillewaet some 3 km (2 miles) away. Almost within sight of the yards, the engineer suddenly slammed on his brakes to avoid another slide. The tender bumped into the engine, permitting the cable hooked over the drawbar to slacken and fall off. Almost before anyone realized what had happened, the tender began to roll down the slope.

The three men on top of the tender suddenly discovered that there was no hand-brake on the car. As one man expressed it: "She was free to go wherever she wanted." With horror in their hearts, Jones and Calder jumped. Sheppherd, whether from fright or hope that a miracle would happen, stayed with the runaway.

Realizing their utter helplessness, the engineer of the auxiliary engine blasted his whistle, hoping the men below would understand that something

Boxcar in a snow cut. In a similar situation the runaway tender instantly killed eleven of fourteen men working in the cut.

was wrong. But the crew in the cut worked on. The five men in the engine cab chatted casually.

Joseph Ditomassi, a trackman working on a shelf above the slide with two companions, noted the engineer's frantic blast. "Guess she must have run into a slide," someone said.

"We heard a whistling sound like another slide coming," said Ditomassi. "Then we saw through the darkness of the night an even darker object approaching along the tracks at terrific speed. We called to those in the deep cut below and to those in the engine to jump, but they didn't have a chance."

Hurtling out of the night, its noise deadened by the falling rain and the light crust of frost on the rails, its approach undetected until the last agonizing moment, the runaway tender crashed into the cut. In a last second effort to escape, men tried to claw their way up the icy walls of the cut.

Joseph Ditomassi and his companions stared in shocked disbelief.

Of the five men trapped in the locomotive cab, Haug and Roland were killed instantly. Dick Cossar was hurled against the water glass which broke and gushed scalding water over him. Alexander and Shafer were knocked down, Alexander suffering a badly broken foot and Shafer a severe chest injury. Only E. G. Bowie, a mechanic who was standing by the engine, escaped without injury.

Of the fourteen men working in the cut, eleven died instantly and the others suffered severe injuries. When the rescue crew arrived they found the dazed survivors attempting to rescue the men still trapped inside the almost crushed locomotive cab. The six badly injured men were carried over the slide and sped towards Revelstoke by special train. Early in the morning, Dick Cossar died in Revelstoke hospital.

Andrew Sheppherd, last seen riding the runaway tender, was not found until the following day. He had waited too long to jump and when he did, broke his neck when he hit the retaining wall of an 18-meter (60-ft.) embankment. He was the fifteenth casualty.

The snow-ridden mountain slopes threatened further destruction as the rain and thaw continued through March 3rd. A huge rotary plow was thrown off the track and engineer Roy McKay suffered a fractured leg. Passenger train No. 4 from Vancouver had windows and vestibules smashed by a series of small slides as it crawled through the area but no one was injured. At another place two cars were derailed. Traffic was halted until the numerous slides were cleared, with nearly 100 eastbound passengers stranded in Revelstoke alone. Elsewhere, two other passenger trains and several freights were sidelined until the danger passed.

In 1937, as if determined to drive the railroad completely out of the Selkirks, the avalanches bombarded the line once more. Experienced engineers such as George Williamson, Walter Pavey and James Carmichael, who operated the pusher engines or the massive rotary plows, became adept at detecting slides and using evasive tactics. Whenever on a slide job, they kept their hands on the controls and a weather-eye cocked to the mountainsides.

On a March afternoon in 1937, a slide came down near Laurie Tunnel and a crew under engineer Carmichael moved in from Revelstoke to clear it.

To challenge Rogers Pass, one of the toughest sections of railway in the world, between 1929-50 the CPR built 35 locomotives which were among the world's largest. Each was over 30 m long (nearly 100 feet), weighed over 700,000 pounds and carried 12,000 gallons of water and 5,000 gallons of fuel. By contrast, the famous World War Two Lancaster bomber carried just over 2,000 gallons.

Their unit consisted of a rotary plow in front, a pusher engine and two cabooses. It was a relatively light slide and since it had not frozen, offered little resistance to clearing.

Conductor Jack Macdonald, a skilled engineer and after whom the present Jack Macdonald avalanche shed is named, traded places with Carmichael, who returned to the caboose for a cup of coffee. A trainman saw a slide start down the mountain and, realizing that Macdonald could not see it because of the snow flying around the rotary plow, pulled the emergency cord.

The slide hurtled down to the river, passing just in front of the rotary. The entire crew breathed a gusty sigh of relief as they watched the mass of snow career up the opposite valley wall. Then, to their horror, the avalanche slowed, made a half circle and hurtled upwards towards them. Such was the bulk and momentum of the snow that it toppled the engine and cabooses off the track into the river, but left the rotary plow still on the track.

Unhurt but shaken, the crew rushed to the overturned engine to rescue Macdonald, but were driven back by a second, smaller slide. Then a third

buried the engine under some 15 meters (50 ft.) of snow. It was four days before Macdonald's body was recovered.

A New Era: The Gas Engine

By the middle of World War One, motorized transport began to appear and, despite early ridicule, by the Twenties it was obvious that the automobile and truck were here to stay. Gradually, like the fur trader and the miner, the Fords, the McLaughlins and the Mitchell Sixes began nosing the toes of the Selkirks. Finding no passage, they turned southward through the Crowsnest Pass and the United States to gain entry into British Columbia.

As early as 1924, the B.C. government began looking at the Selkirks for a possible route between east and west. It looked hopefully for the motor car, unlike the ponderous locomotive, did not need such smooth inclines or extended turns. Again, however, the Selkirks denied them access. They eventually settled for a route which followed the Columbia River some 150 km (90 miles) north from Revelstoke and 160 km (96 miles) southeastward to Golden. Construction began in 1928 and, in 1929, Dominion engineers commenced work on the eastern section from Donald. In 1934, construction was taken over by Federal-Provincial Relief Projects and within the next six years an estimated $3 million was spent, a massive sum in those depression years. The Big Bend opened in 1940 but because World War Two had erupted, the event went virtually unnoticed.

The Big Bend Highway was never quite finished. It was a six-hour trip by car — if the driver was lucky. When a roadside sign said "15 miles per hour" it meant exactly that. It was a fair-weather road, never paved, and although a battery of graders patrolled it almost constantly, it remained a dusty, pot-holed, lonely thoroughfare. Travellers used to stop frequently to tighten bolts and dentures.

Then in 1953 Rogers Pass, which for almost forty years had been left free to play its annual game of spring bowling with the remnants of the old CPR snowsheds, was invaded once again. Federal Department of Public Works snow research stations were established and revealed that there were seventy-four danger areas in the section from which avalanches normally fell. While the average snowfall was an astonishing 900 cm (350 inches) — of itself a not insurmountable problem — studies indicated that the snow tended to settle in specific areas and that unseasonal thaws, or wind erosion, precipitated most of the slides. These slides themselves were of three basic types.

The first group was composed of brittle snow that refused to cling long to the slopes and slithered down, usually harmlessly. Another type was formed by a mass of hard snow breaking off and, like a snowball, gathering more snow on its rush down the mountainside. The last group, and the most dangerous, was caused by massive ledges of snow-turned-ice which built up so that weight alone caused it to break loose and plummet to the valley floor, carrying rocks, uprooted trees and other debris. An added danger was that years of avalanche action — especially on Mount Avalanche — had left the mountainsides smooth with nothing to deter or even slow the speed of the slide.

While the avalanche study was still underway, the B.C. government decided to abandon the Big Bend Highway as a part of the Trans-Canada system and settled on Rogers Pass. In 1956 an observation center was established on Mount Abbott and a new concept of avalanche protection evolved.

Starting high on the mountainside, engineers sought out natural plateaus and widened them to catch slides early. Lower down, following the path of slides, they built mounds of rubble to slow down and break up the avalanche should it reach the lower regions. Finally, at road level, a series of snowsheds was planned to carry the snow over the highway. Buffers were to be installed immediately above these sheds to channel the avalanches over the tops.

To prevent the build-up of massive avalanches whose destructive forces were far greater than man could defend against, a program of deliberate slide precipitation was planned. By using howitzers, build-ups could be shelled and dislodged before they reached dangerous proportions. The engineers trusted their system of defence to dispel the resulting slide harmlessly before it reached the highway or railroad.

In 1958, surveyors moved into the Rogers Pass and in 1959 the roadbuilders came. They were a different breed from those who had descended upon Rogers Pass in 1884-85. Gone were the pick and shovel; gone were the horse drawn graders and scrapers; gone the ponderous old steam-driven piledrivers. In their places were powerful Euclids, powerdriven scrapers, bulldozers. In 1885, a good man with a pick was described as a one who could "keep only two good shovellers going." In 1960, a modern Euclid could scoop up the work of those old-time pickers and shovellers in one gulp of its cavernous jaws. In 1885, a man's worth was measured in brawn, an ability to live with danger day in and day out, and a measure of raucous humor. The new Rogers Pass man was measured by his ability to handle ponderous machines, his record of safety, and his adeptness at brightening the lives of the damsels of Revelstoke and Golden.

A highway 147 km (92 miles) long was pushed through the Selkirks, in many places utilizing the original roadbed established by the railroad. East of the summit, the highway engineers uncovered the remains of the CPR roundhouse destroyed by an avalanche in 1899. At the summit the highway passes over Connaught Tunnel which railway engineers built to thwart the avalanches.

The most difficult problem was the nature of the rock in the Selkirks. The Selkirk Range is older than the Rockies to the east by several million years and weather conditions have eroded its slopes and weathered its rocks, to a much greater extent. Where normal rock blasting produces fragmented pieces, the same procedures in the Selkirks was apt to split enormous slabs of rock off the mountain. There were several delays before a new technique of blasting proved effective. Simultaneous with the road building went the construction of snowsheds. The largest, the Lanark, is 360 meters (1,200 ft.) long and cost close to $700 a meter.

Finally on July 31, 1962, the Honorable W. A. C. Bennett, Premier of British Columbia, cut a ribbon and a cavalcade of cars bearing an estimated 7,000 people streamed over Rogers Pass. But that wasn't the end of pomp and ceremony. Politics demanded a second opening. On September 3, 1962, the Prime Minister of Canada, the Right Honorable John G. Diefenbaker, officially opened the highway on behalf of the federal government. It seemed only right that such a rugged protagonist as Rogers Pass be honored with two official ceremonies.

"Such a view! Never to be forgotten!" wrote young Albert Rogers eighty-one years before, as he saw Rogers Pass with his famous uncle, Major Rogers. "Our eyesight caromed from one bold peak to another for miles in all directions.... Everything was covered with a shroud of white, giving the whole landscape the appearance of snow-clad desolation."

Perhaps some of young Roger's descendents will journey through Rogers Pass in the summer when the region is a swirling mass of green grass and rainbow-hued flowers; when brown and black bears saunter down the railroad tracks in search of berries; when the black ribbon of asphalt lies across the valley like a necklace dotted with multi-colored beads of cars; and when the monument at the summit is surrounded by gaily-decked tourists clicking their camera shutters in rapture.

They will undoubtedly endorse the sentiments of their pathfinding forebear: "Such a view. Never to be forgotten!"

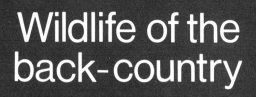

Wildlife of the back-country

by ED CESAR

In national parks such as Glacier, Banff, Jasper and others in the west the average visitor can expect to see bighorn sheep, deer, elk and smaller wildlife, including curious chipmunks and squirrels which frequent the campsites. Most visitors, however, seldom see the animals which shun regions where people are active. Backpackers and hikers are more likely to see wolverine, flying squirrels, pikas, marmots and other wildlife which live in the deep woods or high on the mountains.

During several decades of wresting a living from the wilderness by wildlife photography and live trapping animals, I have been able to photograph most kinds of wildlife, but not without complications and not always in harmony with all of nature's creatures. One of them in particular — the spiny porcupine — has been my wilderness cross for many years. The reason is his eating habits. Although the usual diet of this mobile pin cushion is bark, twigs, birds and leaves, almost every sportsman has some story to tell of the animal's weird and varied appetite, especially his love affair with axe handles.

One summer, for instance, I built a little plywood shack at the end of my trapline and stocked it with campstove, dishes and firewood, ready for an occasional stopover during the winter months. But, on approaching the shack that winter, I discovered some porcupines had reduced it to little more than a roof and parts of the walls which stood on stilt-like, two-by-four studdings. During the summer and autumn the animals had eaten the plywood as high as they could reach, then taken advantage of the deepening snow to gobble even higher.

I rebuilt the shack the following summer, this time covering the bottom half of the outside walls with heavy gauge tin. I left with the assurance that it was now definitely porcupine proof. But the supposedly dull-witted animals were not outdone. On returning to the shack the next winter, I found the walls intact but the roof riddled with gaping holes. The porcupines had climbed along an overhanging limb of a nearby tree and simply dropped onto the roof. Their departure was equally simple — they just dropped from the roof to the ground.

The porcupine is fond of anything that is hard, tough and constipating, preferably axe and shovel handles which have been impregnated with salt from human perspiration. One porcupine, however, really astonished me with his appetite.

I once used a small rubber-tired tractor fitted with a set of tracks which connected the front and back wheels. While the machine sat unused, a porky went to work on the inch-deep rubber lugs of the back drive-wheels. Sitting on the bottom inside of one set of tracks, it had nibbled away on the lugs as high as it could reach, then ambled to the other side and chewed those lugs flush with the face of the tire. It must have swallowed every bit of the rubber for there was not a trace lying around.

The result of this gustatory activity was that ever after the tractor had a most erratic gait. At a fast pace, with the lugless parts in corresponding positions, I would gradually find myself not sitting in the seat but "posting" like an English horseback rider. With the depressions in opposite positions, the motion was like that of a waddling duck. I could not thereafter use the machine without harboring black thoughts against the prickly fellow.

To the casual observer the porcupine may appear to be something of a villain, capable of inflicting lengthy suffering and even death by a mere swipe of its quill-studded tail. Actually, porky is a dull, peace-loving fellow strictly on the defensive and quite harmless if left alone. It is only when approached or threatened that its arsenal of some 30,000 needle-sharp,

One species seldom seen by highway travellers is the flying squirrel, although it glides rather than flies. As shown at left, between its front and back legs and its body are membranes which it tightens once airborne, making an ideal gliding surface. The flying squirrel can travel up to 90 m (300 ft.) if conditions are right. In landing, the squirrel twists its body upward to reduce speed and extends its legs to absorb the shock, using its flat tail as a stablizer.

bristling quills present an ominous and ample warning. It is as emphatic a "go away" as one will ever experience.

In an "on guard" position the porcupine arches its back, bringing every quill bristling erect, presents its rear to the enemy and lashes out with its club-like tail. Because the quills are loosely rooted one occasionally shakes free from the tail during vigorous action, giving rise to the belief that the animal can "shoot" its quills at an attacker. Actually, direct bodily contact must be made to drive the shafts home, either by the attacker bumping into the quills or receiving them by way of a slap of the tail.

The yellowish-white 5 to 7.5 cm (2 to 3 ins.) quill is needle sharp on the business end while the other end is blunt and loosely attached to muscles just under the skin. The sharp end is covered with microscopic scales which lie flat against the quill until it becomes embedded in an attacker's flesh. There it becomes a one-way missile, working forward deep into the muscle tissue and can only be pulled out backwards, even then with difficulty.

The porcupine, whose name comes from the French and means "spiny pig," has black hair which mixed with the yellowish-white quills gives a black and white appearance. Found in both mountain and plains areas, it is equally at home on the ground or on the branches of trees, although its den is usually located in a hollow log or under the roots of a large tree. The young, usually only one, is born in May or June, its quills already developed but soft and pliable until exposed to air.

In contrast to my experiences with porcupines, my encounters with the Canada lynx have usually been enjoyable. Ranging over most of the north and throughout the Rockies, the lynx, with its long legs, big feet, short chunky body, elevated posterior and short bobbed tail, presents a bizarre appearance. While lacking in conventional feline grace, its head with imposing side ruffs, baleful green eyes and stiff black tufts rising from sharp pointed ears is far more impressive than that of a cat.

During winter the lynx's large round feet become heavily furred for support in the deep snow of its forest habitat. Its favorite prey, the varying hare, is equally endowed and can dart over the snow five to ten miles an hour faster. The lynx, however, compensates for these mathematical odds by surprise attacks. It crouches alongside an established "run" and pounces on the hare as it hops by, or springs on it from the lower branches of a tree.

Most cats dislike water but not the lynx. I have seen one unhesitatingly jump into a river, swim to the other side and continue on its way. Old-timers and guides confirm that these animals do not mind the water. They have seen them floating on logs and other objects, apparently enjoying a pleasant cruise down the river.

The lynx, in its natural habitat and under normal circumstances, is usually nocturnal. It hunts in daylight only when very hungry or bored. Its eyes are designed by nature to enable it to track down quarry in almost total darkness. During daylight hours the pupils are scarcely more than slits. As light ebbs the irises open until the pupils nearly fill the eyes and glow ominously in the dark. The eyes, however, do not generate any light themselves. They merely reflect whatever light is present in the gloom. Behind this remarkable power lies an interesting fact. The inner wall of the eye is coated with a substance called "guanin" which has a metallic lustre of silver or gold and brightens dimly-lit images on the retina, enabling the lynx to see them better.

The mating period of the lynx's life is lusty and loud. The animals give vent to a series of shrieks and wails in hair-raising volume. In fact, they make the duet of a pair of courting house tabbies sound like a lullaby. Many a novice woodsman — including me — has been driven to the verge of panic by their unearthly shrieks. My first experience was as a teenager spending a few days with my uncle on his trapline. At dusk one evening as we snowshoed along I suddenly froze, petrified with terror. From the gloom of the darkening woods came an eerie, loud caterwauling unlike anything I had ever heard before. My uncle paused for a moment then continued on his way. "Nothing to worry about," he said casually, "just a tom lynx out a-courting."

The young — up to five kittens — are born in the spring in a hollow log or cavity. At birth their eyes are open, they can stand in two hours and soon after stagger around the den. They are weaned in three months, after which time they pad after mother on her hunting forays. Birth spots and bands give way to long, grey fur mixed with black and brown, and by midwinter the young are grown and fend for themselves.

When seen in the wilderness the lynx appears much larger than its actual 20 to 30 pounds. French-Canadians call it "loup cervier" — the wolf which kills deer. Similar accusations come from other sources but I believe that killing a deer is beyond the capability of such a relatively small animal. A lynx might jump a small fawn or administer the death blow to a sick or nearly starved adult caught floundering in a snowdrift, but a mature, healthy deer is quite safe.

Another animal whose prowess is overrated by many is the wolverine. It is hated and feared because of its reputation as a rapacious killer and a deliberate destroyer. I have found, however, from years of live trapping and photographing the animals that this reputation is not totally warranted. The wolverine does not kill capriciously. It kills to satisfy a voracious appetite caused by its highly efficient digestive system.

In its search for sustenance the animal ranges over a wide territory, hunting almost constantly for its usual diet of mice, groundsquirrels, hares, chipmunks, birds and carrion. An animal of great courage, the wolverine, when occasion warrants, will challenge animals much larger than itself for their kills or caches. Folklore attributes the wolverine with being able to drive wolves and even bears from their food. I think this belief is somewhat exaggerated. On my trapline, however, I filmed a wolverine confronting two coyotes at the remains of a winter-killed moose. The coyotes disputed the intrusion for a few moments then hastily retreated, even though each was larger than the wolverine.

The wolverine's constant search for food often results in its reprehensible habit of robbing traps on traplines. This habit has probably been responsible for many stories about the animal. Often those wolverines to whom unusual prowess is attributed are ones which have been trapped and then escaped. From the experience they develop such cunning for evading traps and a propensity for looting that their abilities cause men to have a superstitious fear of them.

A wolverine comes upon two coyotes feeding on a moose hide. One leaves but the other decides to defend his lunch. The wolverine quickly convinces him otherwise.

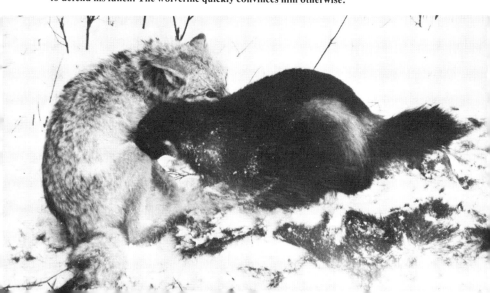

Found mainly in forested wilderness areas at altitudes over 1,200 m (4,000 ft.) the wolverine is the largest member of the weasel family. It has a thick-set, powerful body, strong legs and a short bushy tail. Its somewhat stiff fur is a glossy dark brown with a yellowish-grey band extending over the rump and along the sides. The animal has no enemies other than man who uses its pelt for parka trimmings because the fur does not frost up.

From two to four creamy white young are born in an improvised snow cave or sheltered cranny, usually in mid-February. How long the young stay with their mother is unknown but it is assumed that by fall they are two-thirds grown and ready to be on their own.

The wolverine is a remarkable animal, but so are many other inhabitants of the back country. One creature that always fascinates me is the pika. I have spent many hours observing this alpine inhabitant on wind-blown mountain crests in a labyrinth of rocks and boulders where the tiny pika spends the summer months busily laying up forage for the winter. Unlike its more fortunate neighbors — the hoary marmot, the golden mantled groundsquirrel and chipmunk which hibernate — the pika remains relatively active the year round. Hence produce must be stored to satisfy its vegetarian appetite while the lofty crags are buried deep in snow.

Back and forth over the talus slopes the animals scuttle between their rockslide dens and patches of alpine vegetation. Clipping all they can carry crossways in their mouths, they scamper home. Here they spread the vegetation to cure in the sun on a slab, then hurry back for more. Should rain threaten the little fellows bustle about getting their harvest under cover where it remains until dry conditions again prevail. Then it is once more spread out. As portions cure and are deemed ready for storage, they are stacked into a hay mow, usually between boulders roofed by overhanging rocks. Occasionally the hay is stacked into two or sometimes three smaller lots within a few yards of each other. The animals' judgment of a proper shelter for their crops and their ability to cure vegetation to perfection is shown by the sweetness and freshness of the vegetation the following spring.

By autumn a group of pikas might boast a 50-pound hay mow — an incredible amount of work for an animal that weighs between four and six ounces. Although the contents are mainly grasses, it can include goldenrod, fireweed, berries, herbs and leaves and thistles, a favorite food. Then, regardless of the depth of snow or cruel gales above, the little animals live through the long winter months in comfort.

A group of pikas consists of six to nine and lives more or less permanently in one area, usually no closer than 150 yards from another group. The young are born in the first part of June, usually two, sometimes three and rarely four to a litter, and are nearly mature in two months.

The pika's scientific name *Ochotona* means "short-eared rabbit without a tail." The animal is also referred to by several other names — the cony, rock rabbit, whistling hare and little chief hare. But this animated bit of grey-brown fluff has little in common with a rabbit except for a double set of upper incisors. Its hind legs are no longer than its front, so it scurries rather than hops; its ears are short and round; and it is tailless. And, unlike the rabbit, it lives on mountain crests in western and northwestern North

America at altitudes of 2,400 m to 4,000 m (8,000 to 13,600 ft.), from northern New Mexico in the south to the region of Alaska's Mount McKinley in the north. Regardless of its location, the pika's innate instinct to gather, cure and store alpine vegetation is believed to be basically the same.

Another animal of the high country is the hoary marmot. While photographing above timberline I always enjoy pausing in alpine valleys and rocky slopes which echo with high-pitched whistles — the sign that a community of hoary marmots is resident. These social animals seem to communicate with each other by "calling and answering" whistles, and they post sentinels in prominent places to give warning whenever an intruder approaches.

With sentinels posted the rest of the community can feed on grasses, flowers, roots and berries which grow in abundance during the short alpine summer, or sun themselves on rocky ledges. But the sentinels' vigilance is not always protection against predators. The marmot's two worst enemies

Pikas gathering their winter food. Although the little animals weigh only four to six ounces, by autumn a colony can harvest and cure a remarkable fifty pounds of hay. They have made homes among the rocks of abandoned CPR snowsheds, including the one at Tractor Sheds Picnic Site. (See page 58.)

are the eagle and the grizzly, a persistent adversary. I have seen areas torn apart, with boulders tossed about and the earth disturbed as though a bulldozer had been at work — evidence of a grizzly's determination to have marmot for dinner.

The marmots live at altitudes of 2,040 m to 2,400 m (6,800 to 8,000 ft.) and dig their burrows deep under rocks rolled onto alpine meadows by rock slides, or under piles of rocks strewn on mountain sides. They have stout bodies, short legs and short bushy tails. Their color — greyish white with black tipped hairs — gives a grizzled appearance and enables them to blend with the rocks. As the animals age they become lighter in color.

During the summer and early fall marmots eat large quantities of food to build up a thick layer of insulating fat needed for their six-month-long hibernation. Prior to hibernating they become very busy, digging below frost level, enlarging and repairing their winter quarters which are then lined with fresh hay. Before hibernation they eat only laxative herbs to cleanse their systems of all food and they require no further nourishment until spring. When they retire to their hay-lined nests in September or October, entrances are closed with plugs of hardened mud pierced by hollow-stemmed grasses to admit sufficient oxygen but keep out the frost.

Once snug in their communal dens they drop into a deep sleep that lasts until April or May. A few days after they curl up their body temperature drops from 37 °C (98.6 °F) to as low as 3 °C (37 °F) and reflexes and sensations gradually disappear. Their heart slackens from eighty beats a minute to one; respiration dwindles to a slow, deep intake of breath every three minutes; and muscles tighten into vise-like stiffness.

Soon after the animals emerge from hibernation four or five young are born in May or June, and are out playing on the rocks about six weeks later. They are apparently one-quarter grown at this time and will remain in the family group until they are a year old.

While I enjoy photographing marmots, one of my favorite subjects was a weasel, affectionately called Willy by my family. Willy was once a regular visitor to my trapline cabin and came and went as he pleased. If the door was open and everyone sat still he would fearlessly enter and examine the interior. He became so accustomed to us that he was easily enticed by a bit of fresh meat to a particular area to be photographed.

(Editor's Note: Willy, sleek and white in his winter coat, is on the inside back cover of this book.)

Willy was a short-tailed weasel, known in his winter coat as an ermine. There are several species of these animals, ranging in size from the two-ounce least weasel to the nine-ounce long tailed weasel, found throughout North America.

Although these species differ in some respects — size and color for instance — they are basically the same and all are frenetic in their constant search for food. They dart, bound, and scurry, never seeming to rest. In spite of their size they will attack anything from a mouse to a varying hare, even though the hare outweighs them many times. Much of their daring and aggressiveness is due to the fact that they require up to forty per cent of their body weight in food every day. And most of this food must be meat because they are the most carnivorous of the *Mustala* family. Although

The Canada lynx has large, furred feet which are excellent snowshoes.

weasels have the reputation of being wanton killers, they usually store surplus food for future use.

The weasel's long, thin, sinuous body is perfectly shaped to enable it to enter the burrows of its favorite prey — mice, groundsquirrels, and voles — and its speed and agility make it a difficult attacker to elude. Often a weasel will make its home in the burrow of a chipmunk or golden-mantled ground squirrel which it has evicted or killed. This den, or burrow, will be located in the weasel's "territory," usually an area of two or three acres depending on the supply of food.

Mating probably takes place in mid-summer but, as in many other musteloids, there is a long period between fertilization of the ovum and its implantation. The young, usually six or seven, are not born until the following April or May. They weigh less than an ounce at birth and their chances of survival are slim. Once past the critical stage, however, they develop rapidly. At five weeks their eyes are open and the mother has weaned them. Two months after birth the fully furred young are following mother on food forays.

In both winter and summer weasels have almost perfect camouflage because their coats blend into the countryside. In fall when days begin to shorten the amount of light received through their eyes is believed to influence the pituitary gland. This gland affects the hormones which control the molting process and animals gradually exchange their rich brown coats for wintery white ones. In March or April the process reverses and the white coat is exchanged for brown. All weasels, except the least weasel, have a black tip on the end of their tail in both winter and summer.

In addition to the photo of Willy which has appeared in many magazines and books, I am extremely fortunate to have photographs of the flying squirrel. This animal, although quite numerous in wooded sections of the Rocky Mountains and northern areas, is seldom seen. Strictly nocturnal, it sleeps throughout daylight in a hollow log or similar shelter and becomes active only during late twilight and darkness. Chances are that the closest encounter most campers have had with this little cousin of the red and the grey squirrel has been a soft thump at night followed by the patter of tiny feet on their tent or trailer.

The flying squirrel I photographed was one of two that were found while very young, by a rancher, in an old tree which had blown over. Reared by kindly hands, the animals became very tame and friendly. Upon reaching maturity, they were set free in the surrounding woods. Human hospitality remained to their liking, however, and the two returned fairly regularly during twilight hours for a handout. Their docility and tolerance for human foibles enabled me to photograph several phases of their glide by inducing them to leap repeatedly to a designated spot baited with their favorite food.

Although the animal is called a flying squirrel, it cannot actually fly but is rather a first class glider. In place of wings it has folds of loose membrane attached to the sides of its body between fore and hind limbs. When it spreads its limbs these folds are stretched out tight, making a wonderful gliding surface. Assisted further by its flat, wide tail the animal glides, or volplanes, usually launching itself on its aerial expeditions from the top of one tree to the base of another. It can cover a remarkable 90 m (100 yards) if the height of the launching and the velocity of the wind is favorable.

Moving in for a landing in its aerial maneuvers, the squirrel steers to a predetermined landing place by raising or lowering its fore limbs to warp its flattened form. The squirrel's flat tail acts as a stabilizer as it twists its body upward in order to break its speed and land upright. An instant before landing its tail drops, the animal swings up to check speed, and extends its legs to absorb the shock.

The flying squirrel's fur is grey above, white underneath with delicate buff on the flanks and soft and fine, quite unlike that of any other Canadian mammal. When the animal is at rest, sitting with fore and hind legs enclosed in the loose skin, the gliding membrane hangs in loose, voluminous folds. It makes the animal appear pudgy, as if its coat were much too large. But when the limbs are extended and the membrane is stretched in flight, the squirrel flattens almost into a square.

This elusive creature dens in hollow trees or abandoned woodpecker nests. A litter of three to six is usually born in May or June. For the first ten days the young are blind and naked but soon after their eyes open and they become fully furred. They are probably on their own by late summer.

Unlike red squirrels, flying squirrels do not gather and store food for winter but must forage nightly for their diet of seeds, berries, buds, and meat when they can get it. They do not hibernate but remain active even in the coldest weather.

Another fascinating animal which remains active despite the elements is the marten, a cousin of the weasel. I first encountered one when a companion and I were snowshoeing along a trail and saw a partially devoured snowshoe hare at the base of a large spruce tree. As we inspected the carcass a marten suddenly vented defiance at us from the branches above. This was indeed a rare sight since these 75 cm (30 ins.) long, reddish-brown, weasel-like creatures are normally very shy and avoid men.

Like all members of the weasel family, the marten is a ceaseless hunter, constantly on the look out for food but seldom killing more than it can eat. On the rare occasion when it cannot finish a kill in one sitting, it will drag the remains under some concealment and stay nearby to feed again. Mainly nocturnal hunters, in summer they spend most of their waking hours in the treetops pursuing red squirrels, their favorite prey. During winter months they spend more time hunting on the ground.

The marten's home is mature evergreen forests at elevations from 1,200 to 2,100 m (4,000 to 7,000 ft.). Its population is cyclic, depending on the corresponding populations of red squirrels, mice and shrews. Although this population trend seems true, the marten does not depend entirely on these animals for food. Its diet also includes grouse, hares, voles, and occasionally some vegetable matter such as berries and pine cone seeds. This latter habit is one reason why the animal is sometimes called a pine marten.

Because of its speed and alertness, the marten's few enemies include only the fisher, lynx and great horned owl. Its main predator is man who traps about 70,000 every winter for their silky, lustrous brown fur.

Male and female martens are normally very hostile toward each other but this hostility ceases during the July mating season when the male is decked in fluffy courting pelage. Scent from his powerful musk glands attracts the female and courting begins. About nine months later three or four fuzzy yellow young, weighing one-half ounce each, are born in a den concealed in a hollow tree or log. In five or six weeks their eyes open and they graduate to solid foods. Soon the young martens become active, tumbling and playing in the den and later chasing one another through the treetops in preparation for the time when they must get their own prey. They will remain with their mother until they are full grown and weigh up to four pounds.

At the beginning of this article I mentioned that during several decades of earning a living by wildlife photography, I found the porcupine a wilderness cross to bear. Porky, however, isn't the most frustrating problem. Nor is the weather, although it is annoying to sit for hours then at the crucial moment have a patch of cloud obscure the subject or rain blot out a shot that might have eluded the photographer for days.

No, neither porky nor the weather are the most frustrating problems. People are! With today's interest in the outdoors, at all seasons the woods are full of fishermen, hunters, hikers, campers and cross-country skiers. Consequently, when I am stalking a restless and elusive creature it is not unusual to hear a cheery, "Hi there. What are you after?"

This unwelcome intrusion not only spoils a possible photograph but usually results in detailed questions, including the length of time it takes to get a photograph. I always reply that there is no set length, there are too many variables — it can take an hour, a day, a week, a month or longer.

But in addition to the people, porcupines and the weather there are other complications when stalking wildlife with a camera. Sometimes other animals, birds or one's own mistakes are the culprits. For instance, I started by believing that tactics learned in years of fur trapping could be adapted to wildlife photography. This theory eventually proved correct and quite successful, but some of the early difficulties were ludicrous and exasperating.

My first camera, a 35mm, took a brunt of miscalculations throughout its brief period of service. On my initital attempt I attached the camera, along with its flash unit, to a little wooden platform and focussed onto a piece of meat beside a game trail. A length of fishline connected the bait to an apparatus that released the camera shutter. Then I covered all but the face of the camera and the flash unit with a small tarpaulin and snow, and left it to its task.

When I returned the camera was gone. The evidence indicated that a large bird, apparently an eagle, had swooped down and swallowed the bait. A long furrow in the snow, gradually diminishing to nothing, indicated that the bird had had difficulty becoming airborne with the camera, flash unit and platform. It had finally gotten its cargo into the air but not for long. The camera was entangled in the uppermost branches of a willow bush and the line had broken, leaving an undoubtedly rattled bird to fly on its way.

On another occasion I constructed a similar set on the edge of a snow-covered swamp, overlooking a run used by snowshoe hares. This time I arranged a triggering mechanism on the trail so that an animal hitting it with a foot or stepping on it would activate the camera shutter. The first picture taken was a success, then occurred another offbeat episode. A moose had browsed his fill in a willow thicket not far away and, out of 360 degrees in which to turn, chose the direction which led to my camera. Not deterred by the alien object, he plowed directly over it, leaving it completely buried under the snow.

Moose are unpredictable in another way. I once equalled, if not shattered, the world track record for the 100-yard dash to the nearest tree. I was encouraged every foot by an enraged mother moose — a formidable opponent from which even the grizzly will flee. Once at the tree I bounded into the safety of its limbs in a climbing feat that could be surpassed only by the squirrel.

On another occasion I was taken unawares by a sow grizzly. Since fleeing from a grizzly invites almost certain death, I waited, with fingers crossed. The sow raged and stamped, deciding whether or not to attack to protect her nearby cubs. She finally decided my camera was harmless and let me go my thankful way.

But as hikers and others who venture off the main thoroughfare realize, such incidents are comparatively rare. As compensation there is the unexpected appearance of a wolverine, flying squirrel, pika, weasel or other animals of the deep woods or the mountains — the wildlife of the back country.

Travel Log: Revelstoke to Golden

The Trans-Canada Highway in Rogers Pass. "Our eyesight caromed from one bold peak to another for miles in all directions," Albert Rogers wrote in May 1881, when he and his uncle discovered the pass.

148 Km (92 Miles)

Km 0 - Mile 0

Revelstoke: The history of Revelstoke goes back to the early 1870s when the region was known as "The Eddy" because of a large eddy in the Columbia River. Then during surveys for the Canadian Pacific Railway the name was changed to "Second Crossing" since here the railway would cross the Columbia River for the second time. A third name originated in 1880 when A. S. Farwell laid out a townsite nearby and called it after himself.

Farwell developed as a typical frontier community. Colonel Edward Mallandaine who operated a pony express carrying mail west to Eagle Pass Landing wrote that in 1888 Farwell "...consisted of one street, on either side of which were wooden and log shacks, chief among them the Columbia Hotel.

"In Farwell, as at Eagle Pass Landing, the life was exciting, especially on pay days. There were brawls continually and gambling night and day with men of all nationalities throwing away their hard-earned pay at faro, stud poker and other games of chance. What the gamblers and saloon men did not get, the women of the town did, and a very small proportion of the money reached storekeepers."

Farwell, however, was not destined to survive. Its promoter felt that the CPR had no choice other than to run its line through his townsite. He upped the price of land accordingly. For its part the CPR didn't agree and laid out its own townsite which it called Revelstoke. The bypassed Farwell soon faded into memory.

46

Revelstoke became an important railway divisional point and a major supply base for the Arrow Lakes and West Kootenay region to the south. For many years it was a port of call for the colorful sternwheel steamers which plied Arrow Lakes and the Columbia River. Today it has a population of some 10,000 and all visitor services, including an excellent museum.

Route mileage starts at Woodenhead Park on the Trans-Canada Highway just over the Columbia River Bridge. The Park is named after the "wooden head" which is on display. It was carved in 1937-38 by Italian workmen helping to build the Big Bend Highway. For years it was on display at Boat Encampment Lodge near Mica Creek but was removed when the Big Bend closed after completion of the Rogers Pass route.

Km .8 - Mile .5

Junction: Here in a chalet-style hut is Revelstoke's Chamber of Commerce Information Centre which is open during summer. Turn north for Revelstoke and Mica Creek Dams.

Revelstoke Dam is 4 km (2.8 miles) north of the Junction and Mica Dam 136 km (85 miles) north over a paved highway. Both were built as part of the Columbia River treaty between the U.S. and Canada to help control flooding of the Columbia River and to generate power.

Mica is the largest earth-filled dam in North America. It rises some 190 m (650 ft.) above the river bed and is nearly a kilometer (one-half mile) wide.

It created an inland sea which extends from Valemount in the north about 216 km (135 miles) to Donald Station in the south. The dam features a Visitor Centre which is open during the summer with two tours a day.

The Revelstoke Dam, Canada's highest concrete dam and one of North America's largest, is only a few minutes drive north of Revelstoke. It is well worth a visit and features a self-guiding tour with individual "talking wands" which enable visitors to start their tour immediately on arrival. The tour includes an elevator trip to the top of the 175-m- (560-ft.-) high dam, views of the main powerhouse gallery, circuit breaker gallery, and much more. It is open from March to October but visitors should check at the Revelstoke Chamber of Commerce Information Centre before leaving for either dam to confirm Visitor Centre hours.

Overlooking the Columbia River and Revelstoke Dam is Columbia View Provincial Park. It has a shelter with cooking facilities, picnic tables, children's playground and a Stop-of-Interest sign:

"RIVER OF THE WEST: For 1,200 miles, in two countries, the Columbia carves its way to the Pacific Ocean. Named after Robert Gray's ship the *Columbia,* it was first mapped in 1811 by David Thompson. This 'highway' for traders, missionaries and gold miners later became a route for sternwheelers. Dammed for flood control and hydro-electric power the river continues to serve the Pacific Northwest."

Km 1.6 - Mile 1

Junction: Twenty-six–km (15-mile) Summit Road winds upward to Mount Revelstoke National Park in its spectacular setting on 1,805-m (6,350-ft.) Mount Revelstoke. Here visitors can look across meadows of multi-colored alpine flowers while standing in a forest of alpine cedar and hemlock. Also, it is probably the only park in the world from where visitors can see three mountain ranges while sitting in their car. These are the Monashees across the Columbia River to the west; the Selkirk, home of formidable Rogers Pass; and the Clachnacudainn Range to the north.

There are no campgrounds in the park but there are picnic sites and pull-outs along Summit Road. The most spectacular is Monashee Viewpoint at Km 7.5 (Mile 4.6). It includes drinking water, firepits, picnic tables, shelter with stove, and arrows identifying the Monashee Peaks across the Columbia River and points of interest in Revelstoke far below. The highest peak is Mt. Begbie at 2,724 m (nearly 9,000 ft.).

In Mount Revelstoke there are over 65 km (40 miles) of trails, including self-guiding Mountain Meadows at the Summit. This trail loops through sub-alpine meadows in a pleasant 15-minute walk that introduces visitors to a region where summer is about eight weeks long and the Columbian ground squirrels hibernate nine to ten months of the year.

Just below the Summit is a beautiful alpine picnic site on Balsam Lake. It includes tables, shelter with stove and washrooms with flush toilets.

Km 17 - Mile 10.5

48

Illecillewaet Rest Area and Viewpoint overlooking the Illecillewaet River, an Indian word which means, appropriately, fast water. It is pronounced "Illy-silly-what." This is the stream that Walter Moberly followed in 1865 in his unsuccessful attempt to find a route through the Selkirk Mountains. Although he didn't find a pass, he did become one of B.C.'s most prominent pathfinders. In 1865 he discovered Eagle Pass which the CPR and Trans-Canada Highway use to cross the Monashee Mountains, and later selected Burrard Inlet as the western terminal for the CPR. He predicted that a major city would grow at the end of steel and was proved right. Today that city, Vancouver, is the third largest in Canada, center of a population of over two million.

In 1885 about 8 km (5 miles) upstream from the lookout was born the community of Illecillewaet. In his book, *Among the Selkirk Glaciers*, William Spotswood Green described it as a "typical frontier village, the inhabitants being all prospectors, miners, engaged in silver mines, lumber-men, and Canadian Pacific Railway (employees).

"The city seemed to have no plan, but on the map which we saw it was laid out in the most splendid series of lots, and two steamers were represented as plying on the river — which, by the way, is a glacier torrent flowing at about 20 miles per hour."

The houses were wooden and some of them "...stood on legs in swampy pools only half reclaimed from the overflow of the river by piles of empty meat tins, broken packing cases, etc., which were littered about everywhere."

One inn had been closed by the sheriff, for what reason the author didn't mention, although his description of the remaining one provides a good hint. The gentlemen's shaving room turned out to be a wash basin on the stump of a tree, a strip of leather nailed to the side of the building was the razor strop, while a piece of broken mirror completed the fixtures.

At the viewpoint is a Highway's Rest Area with toilets and a cairn which commemorates the B.C. government's "official" opening of the Rogers Pass on July 20, 1962. (Because of inter-government rivalry, the Federal government also held its own "official" opening. (See Km 69.2.)

The inscription on the cairn notes: "Rogers Pass, in the Selkirk Mountains, was discovered by Major A. B. Rogers, Canadian Pacific Railway Mountain Division Chief Engineer, May 25, 1881, with a party of Indians from Kamloops. The following year he crossed through the pass on foot.

"Let all who use this Highway look with awe and reverence upon the majesty of God-given beauty of these mountains."

Km 19 - Mile 11.8
Western Boundary Mount Revelstoke National Park: Eastward the highway traverses the Park for 12 km (7 miles) but there are no facilities. Westbound travellers will find a description of the Park and the scenic drive to its summit at Km 1.6.

Km 27.1 - Mile 16.8
Skunk Cabbage Nature Trail: This self-guiding trail with its boardwalk

over a typical Interior wetbelt swamp can be enjoyed by the entire family in under one-half hour. Descriptive signs along the Trail resemble the pages of a park naturalist's notebook and identify the amazing number of birds, insects and plants. In addition, there is a picnic area on the Illecillewaet River which includes kitchen shelter with stove, tables, flush toilets — and friendly Columbian ground squirrels.

Km 29.9 - Mile 18.5
Giant Cedars Nature Trail: A 15-minute circular hike over a self-guiding boardwalk with descriptive signs which identify species from the massive cedar to thimbleberry, devil's club to early blueberry. And how old are some of the lofty cedars? Well, if you guess 800 or so years you won't be far wrong.

A kitchen shelter with stove, picnic tables and toilets in a woodland clearing with its resident Columbian ground squirrels make Giant Cedars a pleasant stop.

Km 30.7 - Mile 19
Eastern Boundary Mount Revelstoke National Park: For westbound travellers access to this unique park is at Km 1.6.

Km 34.2 - Mile 21.2
Illecillewaet River and Bridge: For eastbound travellers this is the first of several crossings as the highway threads upstream to the summit of Rogers Pass.

Km 34.9 - Mile 21.6
Albert Canyon Hot Springs: These mineral waters were probably discovered by Canadian Pacific Railway workmen who built a timber enclosure at the site of the springs. Today, water is piped over 3 km (about 2 miles) from the springs to two pools. One is a hot pool with a temperature of 40°C (104°F), while the other is a swimming pool with a more comfortable 26°C (80°F). Facilities include licensed restaurant, trading post and campsites in a forest setting. Open from May to September.

Km 46.4 - Mile 28.7
McDonald Avalanche Shed: The most westerly of a series of three snow-sheds which protect the highway from avalanches. Others lower in the valley cover the railway. Above the railway is the remains of a mining venture. In the 1880s near Laurie in the Illecillewaet Valley the Selkirk Mining & Smelting Company struck a lode of silver averaging 70 to 120 ounces per ton of ore. On a grassy flat at the east end of the Illecillewaet Tunnel, a hotel, offices, and manager's residence and a concentrator were built. High on the perpendicular face of the cliff behind was the bunkhouse, near the mouth of the main shaft. From here ore was carried in buckets along a wire cable to the concentrator 900 m (3,000 ft.) below. Although in one place it descended a sheer 450 m (1,500 ft.) to the valley floor, miners ascended and descended in

the buckets. By the turn of the century, however, the ore body was exhausted and the mine abandoned.

Km 49.2 - Mile 30.5

Western Entrance Glacier National Park: This park was established in 1886 and, contrary to common belief is not in the Rockies but in the Columbia Mountains, one of the most rugged areas of Western Canada. Steep-walled peaks, avalanche-scarred valleys and over 100 glaciers make Glacier Park unique. It is aptly named since glaciers cover about 12 per cent of its 1,350 square-kilometer area (500 square miles). These glaciers are maintained by an average annual snowfall of over 9 m (30 ft.), although in 1966-67 over 18 m (60 ft.) fell. In Rogers Pass itself there is often precipitation one out of every two days in summer and daily in winter. This heavy snowfall, combined with the steep mountains which characterize the area, make Glacier one of the most active avalanche zones in the world.

Parks Canada explains the reason for this snowfall as follows:"Mount Revelstoke and Glacier National Parks are in the Columbia Mountains region of British Columbia. High annual precipitation, heavy snowfall and relatively moderate winter temperatures are outstanding characteristics of this interior wet belt.

"The parks are located at a climatological divide, an area where two weather systems meet. The western part of the divide is influenced more by Pacific weather systems (moist and mild in the winter) and the eastern part is influenced more by continental weather systems (dry and cold in winter.)

"Precipitation in the parks is almost always produced by moist air from the Pacific Ocean moving across the Columbias and being forced to rise. As the air is pushed up and over the mountains, it cools and its moisture is released. Neither the Interior Plateau nor the Rocky Mountains receive the tremendous amount of precipitation that the Columbia Mountains do. The plateau is dry because it is low and in the rain-shadow of the coastal mountains. The Rockies are dry because most of the Pacific air's moisture is lost by the time it reaches them."

Parks Canada also explains the reason for a phenomenon which often startles those passing through the Park in early spring or summer — snow that can be red, yellow or pepper-colored.

"During the late spring and summer, the surface of the snowpack frequently turns watermelon red. This red colour is produced by algae belonging to the genus *Chlamydomonas*. As the last remnants of snow disappear from the subalpine, yellow patches occasionally spot the snow's surface. Close inspection will reveal masses of tiny golden snow fleas (*Onychiurus cocklei*). Throughout the winter, a careful observer can find a variety of invertebrates on the snowpack. Masses of tiny black fleas (*Hypogastriura* sp.) sometimes pepper the snow's surface. Snow craneflies (*Chionea* spp.) stride across the snow all winter long."

Because of the massive precipitation, wildlife in Glacier differs from other National Parks in Western Canada. The deep snow and long winters make life difficult for many forms of wildlife. Birds such as Steller's jays, gray jays — the familiar camp robber or whiskey jack — and Clark's nutcrackers remain all year but most other species migrate in winter. While large mammals such as deer and moose are not common, black and grizzly bear are because the park is well suited to these hibernators. Smaller species such as squirrels and marmots which have adapted to the snow by living above it or by hibernating are also abundant.

In the park all points of interest are marked. There are developed campsites and picnic sites along the Trans-Canada Highway and over 160 km (100 miles) of established hiking trails. Hikers, however, should remember to be alert for bears.

Km 49.6 - Mile 30.7

Viewpoint and Picnic Site: This picnic site on the Illecillewaet River includes toilets, tables, drinking water and, as in other picnic sites along the highway, a welcoming committee of Columbian ground squirrels — see Km 55.2 for information on these friendly mountain residents. An interpretive tablet describes the avalanche slope which fronts the picnic site:

"DESTRUCTION AND CREATION: Avalanches are forces of creation as well as destruction. Snowslides on the slope in front of you have cut through the forest and created the sunny, open slopes favoured by many plants and animals. As a result Glacier National Park has more berries and bears, flowers and marmots, grasses and mice.

"Mountain alder thrives here on the avalanche slope. Tough and flexible, it bends under the force of the cascading snow — and survives.

"From here, you see only one-third of the avalanche slope. Each winter an average of 14 slides roar down from high above. Most of these are started by the park avalanche control team."

Just past the entrance to the picnic site, eastbound, is a concrete circle at the edge of the highway. It is the first in a series of positions where artillery is used to trigger avalanches as part of the Highway's winter defence system.

To summer travellers, the most evident of the defences against avalanches are the concrete snowsheds varying in length from 180 m (600 ft.) to nearly 600 m (2,000 ft.), designed to deflect snow over the highway. Other defences which are not so visible include mounds of rubble between 4 to 8 m (15 to 25 ft.) high built in a checkerboard fashion to break up an avalanche and dissipate much of its force. Higher on the mountainsides flat benches, some 300 m (1,000 ft.) long and 45 m (150 ft.) wide, catch and hold lesser snow slides. Other static defences include earthen diversion dams which catch or direct lesser slides, and avalanche warning signs designating danger areas.

Another defence is described by Parks Canada:

"Unlike the original railway the highway is also guarded by a mobile system of defence. Men are employed year-round studying the climate. In winter, they make detailed weather and snowpack observations. Sophisticated remote sensors in special study areas high in the mountains above the pass continually radio weather information to a central forecast headquarters. Avalanche forecasters use this data and their personal experience to predict when avalanches are likely to occur. Under the direction of these forecasters, gate attendants and park wardens warn motorists entering the park of possible avalanche activity on the highway. The forecaster may decide to close the highway and attack the unstable slide areas with artillery.

"Circular gun positions along the road shoulders are used to station a 105 mm howitzer.... Under the direction of the forecaster the army bombards known trigger zones high up the avalanche paths. The shock waves from exploding shells fired by heavy artillery will trigger avalanches when snow conditions are right. With the highway closed the slides can thunder harmlessly down the slopes."

Km 55.2 - Mile 34.2

Picnic Site: A pleasant oasis amidst conifer and deciduous trees with kitchen shelter and stove, picnic tables, toilet and a tablet with illustrations and the inscription:

"COLUMBIAN GROUND SQUIRREL: You will probably hear them before you see them, boldly emitting loud clear chirps. They are Columbian ground squirrels.

"Columbian ground squirrels dig tunnels with up to 20 meters (65 ft.) of combined passages. You can easily spot the main entrance because bare earth surrounds it, but there are many secret entrances for emergencies.

"During the summer ground squirrels eat roots, bulbs, leaves, grasses and seeds. They have to hurry for they have only three to four months to put on

A howitzer manned by army personnel is used to trigger avalanches while they are comparatively small. One of the gun's shells is on display at Parks Canada's Information Centre. (See page 58.)

fat for a long winter sleep. Many die during their long hibernation.

"Ground squirrels will readily share your lunch but their natural diet is healthier. Please do not feed the Columbian ground squirrels or the other animals in our National Parks."

Km 59.7 - Mile 37

Western Portal to the longest railway tunnel in North America. It was completed in 1988 as part of the Canadian Pacific Railway's $600 million program to upgrade its line through Rogers Pass, reducing the grade from 2.2 per cent to 1 per cent. The nearly 15-km (9-mile) tunnel goes through Mount Macdonald and Cheops Mountain, passing 349 m (1,060 ft.) below Rogers Pass Summit. The tunnel includes a massive automatic air ventilation system with a shaft over 8.5 m (over 25 ft.) wide from the tunnel upwards some 350 m (1,064 ft.) to the surface of Cheops Mountain.

Km 61.7 - Mile 38.2

Cougar Creek Hiking Trail. This trail is typical of most in Glacier National Park in that it heads upward into alpine country. It also gives access to the Nakimu Caves, an underground maze that extends some 6 km (3.7 miles), one of Canada's largest. The system, however, is closed to the public.

Km 62.6 - Mile 38.8

Sir Donald Picnic Site and Viewpoint: Picnic tables and toilets in a peaceful setting of trees, shrubs and flowers on the Illecillewaet River with a background of mountains which tower over 3,200 m (10,000 ft.). Includes an interpretive tablet with illustrations and the inscription:

"A CLASSIC OF THE COLUMBIAS: Mount Sir Donald dominates the skyline ahead of you. Its rugged peak and steep walls typify the Columbia Mountains. The Columbia Mountains are bordered by other natural regions equally distinct. While travelling, you might compare these areas to add interest to your trip.

"West of the Columbias, near Salmon Arm, the Interior Plateau begins. This rolling upland resembles a series of low mountain ranges.

"East of the Columbias, past Golden, the Rocky Mountains display broad valleys and mountains shaped like layer cakes and tilted desks. These contrast to the narrow valleys and sharp peaks of the Columbias.

"If in Banff National Park, you might look for Castle Mountain as an example of the Rockies to compare with Mount Sir Donald, a classic of the Columbias."

Km 63.7 - Mile 39.4

Loop Brook Campground: Twenty campsites, each with parking, table, fire pit and firewood. There is also a kitchen shelter and central flush toilets. Just upstream or downstream are access points to Loop Brook Trail. This self-guiding trail is an easy one-hour hike around the famous loop in the original CPR tracks. There are excellent viewpoints on top of stone pillars which once supported the railway tracks and views of sprawling Bonney Glacier. Along the trail interpretive tablets provide background information on the route.

Km 63.9 - Mile 39.5
Loop Brook and Bridge: On the east bank is a parking area with toilets and start of the Loop Brook Trail with an interpretive tablet which includes illustrations and text:

"THE LOOPS: For many years steam locomotives on the mainland of the Canadian Pacific Railway rumbled across these stone pillars. Construction of the railway through these rugged mountains was a constant struggle. In this area, steep-sided valleys and cascading rivers required an intricate series of loops and bridges along the line.

"The loops contained curves equal to several complete circles and allowed the railway to climb into Rogers Pass at a reasonable grade.

"Loop Brook was first bridged at two points in 1885. In 1908 the original wooden trestles were replaced by steel spans resting on stone pillars. Eight years later the C.P.R. abandoned this part of its line and the stone pillars of Loop Brook Valley were left as monuments to the skill of our pioneers."

Km 65.3 - Mile 40.4
Western Boundary of Rogers Pass: The Pass is about 15 km (9 miles) long. (Eastbound travellers see Km 78.9 for background data.)

Km 66.8 - Mile 41.4
Illecillewaet Campground: On the east bank of the river in a spectacular setting of glacial mountains, the campground has 58 campsites, 2 kitchen shelters and flush toilets in an historical setting. Follow the signs to an exhibit near the site of Glacier House, a major CPR hotel at the turn of the century. Other signs lead to Avalanche Crest Trail, this is a three–hour uphill hike for experienced and well–prepared hikers. The end of the trail has excellent views of Rogers Pass, the original CPR line and the Trans–Canada Highway.

Glacier House, opened in 1887, was one of three Swiss-style chalets built by the CPR in the Rockies. It began primarily as a dining room (and six small bedrooms) for passengers on the east- and west-bound trains whose dining cars were too heavy to pull up the steep inclines to the summit of the Selkirks. So popular did Glacier House become that it eventually expanded to 90 rooms and the chalet almost disappeared in a hodge-podge of architecture faintly reminiscent of a Scottish baronial castle and an English Tudor house. Nonetheless, it was "comfortable and homelike" according to one tourist who praised the hospitality of the staff. Unknown, however, is whether he included in his assessment a young man named Charlie whose job was to guard the decorative white stones surrounding the fountain in front of the chalet. Visitors insisted on taking the stones as souvenirs.

Glacier House became noted for its brilliant displays of wildflowers. While botanists crowded the meadows, mountaineers climbed 3,300 m

(10,000 ft.) peaks led by two Swiss guides imported by the CPR in 1899. Visitors less energetic but still venturesome could hire a packhorse and ride the 7-mile trail to Nakimu Caves where a remarkable group of underground caverns were discovered by hunter-prospector Charles "Old Grizzly" Deutschman in 1904. Tours of the caves were so popular that the CPR built a tea-room and a large log cabin for overnight accommodation. Traces of the stone chimney can still be seen.

Other visitors came to hike and photograph the spectacular scenery with their recently invented Kodak Brownies, while more serious photographers could develop their pictures in the hotel's dark room. Those who came to see the much publicized Illecillewaet Glacier could do so with hardly any effort. In 1885 its great white tongue was only a mile from Glacier House, but it was soon evident that the glacier was receding an average 16.5 m (50 ft.) a year. Today it is some 5 km (3 miles) from the site of Glacier House. This factor, as well as the high cost of maintaining Glacier House as a tourist facility, and the lack of road access, contributed to Glacier's decline and eventual closure in 1925. Four years later the hotel was dismantled.

Km 69 - Mile 42.7

Rogers Pass Summit: With an elevation of 1,330 m (4,043 ft.) Rogers Pass isn't the highest on Canada's highway system. But its steep-sided mountains flanking a narrow valley with a massive snowfall and attendant avalanches make it Canada's most difficult pass to maintain in winter. (At Glacier Park's weather station on Mount Fidelity an annual snowfall of 23 m, or 70 feet, has been recorded.)

Km 69.2 - Mile 42.8

Summit Monument: Here occurred the Federal Government's official highway opening in 1962. The Monument is inscribed with details of the project and with its background of spectacular mountain scenery is a favorite photographic stopping place.

From the Monument there is an interesting one-half hour hike over the Abandoned Rails Trail which ends at Rogers Pass Visitor's Centre. Along the way tablets with illustrations and text provide background data. The walk is along the original CPR line at Rogers Pass Summit and features close views of two snowsheds, associated slide paths and the original Rogers Pass townsite.

Rogers Pass townsite was a lonely little outpost of humanity that was headquarters for the engines which assisted trains over the summit. In 1894 it had two hotels, the Queen and the Brunswick — although both were built of canvas — a post office, general store, station, roundhouse and a boarding house. It was also short lived. On January 30, 1899, an avalanche destroyed the community.

The Revelstoke Herald featured a front page story on the disaster, noting: "A Most Shocking Affair - A Snowslide Sweeps Away The Station and Round

Just east of Rogers Pass Summit is the service headquarters for Glacier National Park. Facilities include Glacier Park Lodge and the Park's Information Centre, built to resemble a CPR snowshed of the 1886 era. The Centre and the Lodge are open all year.

Glacier Park Lodge is a beautiful natural stone and wood structure harmonizing with the wilderness surroundings of Glacier National Park. The completely modern luxury hotel is open 24 hours year round, with services that include fuel, groceries, dining room, cafe, lounge and heated swimming pool. Since the Lodge centers a region noted for abundant snowfall, it is becoming increasingly popular for both ski-touring and cross-country skiing. Guide service is available for those unfamiliar with this region whose mountains tower over 3,000 m (10,000 feet) and rival in beauty – some say exceed – those in Jasper or Banff National Parks.

House At Roger's Pass and Buries Eight People Alive — All the Bodies Have Been Found Except One...." Among the dead were the wife and two children of stationmaster Albert Cator. The tragedy was only one of many which would result in over 250 people being killed by avalanches which swooshed down the steep slopes at over 200 km (120 miles) an hour.

Km 70.4 - Mile 43.6

Glacier Park Lodge and Rogers Pass Centre: The lodge features a huge licensed dining room, accommodation, heated swimming pool, service station and other visitor facilities.

Rogers Pass Centre, opposite the Lodge, is an excellent information facility operated by Parks Canada. The impressive building closely resembles a CPR snowshed — in fact it was built with the aid of railway blueprints. In the Centre the story of Rogers Pass is vividly portrayed in huge color photos, wildlife displays, models and a theatre with films shown throughout the day. A park naturalist is on duty to answer questions. Open every day during summer, and weekdays in winter.

Km 73.1 - Mile 45.3

Tractor Sheds Picnic Site and Viewpoint: Picnic tables and toilets amidst the ruins of an old railway snowshed where pikas have a home, a gun position and welcoming Columbian ground squirrels. Two tablets with illustrations and text provide background data:

"ANIMAL MOUNTAINEERS — Mountain goats live in higher places and on steeper terrain than any other large animal in North America. Here you may see them as small white dots on the cliffs and avalanche slopes above you.

"With 300-400 of them in Glacier National Park, they greatly outnumber the park's other large animals. While heavy snowfall makes it extremely difficult for deer, elk, and moose to find food in winter, mountain goats find forage on high windswept ledges.

"Their skill in climbing cliffs also protects them from predators."

"DEFENDING THE HIGHWAY: The Trans-Canada Highway through Rogers Pass is the largest directly controlled avalanche area in the world. Thousands of snow avalanches thunder down the mountain slopes every winter.

"Several methods are used to protect the highway from these dangerous snowslides.

"This concrete circle is one of several gun positions from which selected avalanche paths are stabilized by artillery fire throughout each winter. At critical times a park avalanche forecaster orders the highway closed and directs a special detachment of the Canadian Armed Forces to fire a 105-mm howitzer at known trigger points in the avalanche paths. By centering the gun on these circles and by using reference points such as the small orange cross on the far side of the highway to aim the gun, they can precisely shell targets up to 8 km away — usually during raging snowstorms and at night!

"Down the road you can see another method of defence; the snowshed. These sheds are used at several locations to shield the highway from avalanches.

"Snowsheds were the only defence used by the original railway over Rogers Pass. You can see the remains of an old railway shed at the back of this picnic area."

Km 73.5 - Mile 45.5
Single Bench Snowshed: First in a series of five which protect the highway in the next 3 km (2 miles).

Km 77.8 - Mile 48.2
Viewpoint with descriptive tablet which includes photos, map and text:
" MOUNTAIN BRIDGES: The stone arch across the valley was part of the original C.P.R. through Rogers Pass. You can still trace the old grade leading to the Bridge.

"Deep notches cut by cascading mountain streams were serious obstacles to the railway builders marching up the Beaver River Valley on their way to Rogers Pass. They met this challenge with skill and determination, leaving in their wake some of North America's most spectacular railway bridges.

"The original wooden bridges built in 1885 were replaced over the years with stone and steel structures. In 1916, when the railway was rerouted from Rogers Pass to the newly completed Connaught Tunnel, this stone arch bridge became obsolete. Others, farther down the valley, remain in use to this day."

Km 78.9 - Mile 48.9
Eastern Boundary Rogers Pass: Parking, toilets and descriptive tablet with illustrations and text:
"ENTERING ROGERS PASS: In 1882 Major A. B. Rogers struggled up this valley and first viewed the eastern entrance to Rogers Pass. This completed the explorations which he had started the year before from the west. At last a route had been found across the inhospitable Selkirk Mountains.

"Rogers Pass has played an exciting role in the story of Canadian transportation. In 1885 the country's first trans-continental railway crossed over the Pass. In 1916, the Canadian Pacific Railway completed Canada's then longest railway tunnel, the 8-kilometer Connaught Tunnel, under the Pass. And, in 1962, Canada's first transcontinental highway again made Rogers Pass a vital artery in the lifeline of this country."

Km 80.5 - Mile 49.9
Viewpoint and descriptive tablet with illustrations and text:
"RUGGED MOUNTAINS: Ice has sculpted the mountains of Glacier National Park. The rounded contours of the Purcells in front of you and the steep, craggy Selkirks behind you were both formed by the immense eroding power of glaciers.

"But how can the same force create such contrasting mountains? In the Purcells the bedrock is softer and the mountains lower. The mountains were buried in moving ice which, over time, smoothed and rounded the rock.

"In the harder, higher Selkirks the peaks were not buried. Solitary mountains once protruded from a sea of ice. Glaciers gnawed into mountain sides, creating bowl-shaped cirques and steep, horn-shaped peaks."

Km 83.7 - Mile 51.9
Beaver River and Bridge: Eastbound travellers now follow the Beaver River out of the Selkirk Mountains northward then eastward to the Columbia River. The mountains on the east bank of the Columbia are the Rockies.

Km 89.1 - Mile 55.2
Beaver River Picnic Site with tables and washrooms.

Km 90.6 - Mile 56.1
For many years this was the location of Mountain Creek Campground, Glacier Park's largest with over 300 units, sani-station, flush toilets and other services. Unfortunately, surrounding trees – Western red cedar, hemlock and Douglas fir – proved to be shallow rooted, making them a potential danger in windy weather and the campsite had to be closed.

Km 93.4 - Mile 57.9
Eastern Boundary of Glacier National Park with descriptive tablet containing illustrations and text:

"GLACIER NATIONAL PARK: What's in a name? Ahead of you lies a park with over 400 glaciers. Only two of them are visible from here — but if you could view the park from the air you would see a preserve where perpetual ice or snow covers about 12 per cent of the land.

"Steep mountains, narrow valleys, avalanche slopes and dense forests also characterize the park's 1,350 sq. kilometers. Here the rugged Columbia Mountain landscape produced a vivid human history — one of challenge to mountaineers and struggle for railway and highway operations.

"For the best view of glaciers from the highway, travel 25 km west to the top of the Rogers Pass. You will also find park information there at the Rogers Pass Centre.

"Welcome to Glacier National Park — a park well named!"

This area is the dividing line between Pacific Standard Time and Mountain Standard Time. Eastbound travellers advance watches one hour; westbound, put them back one hour.

Km 93.8 - Mile 58.1
Heather Hill Lookout with a sweeping view of the Beaver River Valley and eastern entrance to Rogers Pass.

Km 113.2 - Mile 70.2

Redgrave Rest Area on both sides of the highway with picnic tables and toilets.

Km 121.4 - Mile 75.3

Columbia River and Bridge: During railway construction in the early 1880s a flourishing settlement appeared on the east bank of the Columbia at this point. Originally known as First Crossing, it then became Columbia Crossing and, finally, Donald. For a time Donald thrived as headquarters for the CPR's Mountain Division but when headquarters moved to Golden, Donald vanished.

A vivid picture of Columbia Crossing appeared in the *Calgary Herald* on November 19, 1884. Written by correspondent Jack Little, who was also in charge of the telegraph office, it carried the headline:

"A MOUNTAIN CITY AS THE MOON SEES IT

"It lightens up some of the grandest works of the Creator; and if it hadn't to lighten up Bob Philips' saloon, and the Cosmopolitan saloon, and the Queen of the West, and the Swede Hotel, and the Italian restaurant, and the French quarter, and all the rest of the gambling, drinking, fighting little mountain town which lies stretched along the frozen bank of the Columbia, where the CPR crosses it first, it would have nothing to regret.

"The Italian saloon: It is a little hut 12 x 16 and it dispenses beer, cigars and something more fiery, in unlimited quantities. The bar-keeper — Saints preserve us! — is a woman — and Saints preserve her! what a woman! There is an accordeon squaking (sic) in a corner. In fact music is the strong feature of the town. On all sides the music of the dice-box and the chips . . . the merry music of the frequent and iniquitous drunk; the music of the dance and the staccato accompaniment of pistol shots; and the eternal music, from the myriad saloons and dives along the street of the scraping fiddle. In the French quarter a dance is going on. The women present are a Kootenai squaw, 'the first white lady that ever struck Cypress', and two or three of the usual type of fallen angels. A gang of men and boys lines the walls, and a couple of lads dance with the damsels in the centre. There (is) a lamentable sense of shame at Columbia Crossing."

Km 131.2 - Mile 81.3

Doyle Creek Rest Area in the Columbia River Valley. The Columbia is born in the Rocky Mountains south of Golden, flows northwestward around the Selkirk Mountains then at the site of Mica Dam angles southward then westward to join the Pacific Ocean at the Washington-Oregon border. It flows some 2,100 km (1,300 miles) and before the era of dam building, salmon in an incredible journey fought upstream to spawn at its headwaters.

Km 136.3 - Mile 84.4

Stop of Interest sign with text:

"RAILWAY SURVEYOR: In 1871, Walter Moberly, in charge of surveys for the mountain division of the projected Canadian trans-continental

Mt. Sir Donald from the Trans-Canada Highway. At 3,289 m (nearly 11,000 feet), it is the highest peak in Rogers Pass.

Travellers with time should consider a drive over pavement to alpine country in Mt. Revelstoke National Park. (See page 48.)

railway, built log cabins east of here for survey party 'S'. The preliminary surveys through Howse Pass were abandoned in 1872 in favour of the Yellowhead route, but in the end the railway used Kicking Horse Pass. Moberly Marsh and Moberly Peak honour this early surveyor in British Columbia."

Eastbound travellers now enter the Rocky Mountains, the Columbia River being the dividing line between the Rocky and the Purcell Mountains on the west bank of the Columbia.

Km 148 - Mile 92

Golden: A modern community with a population of 3,500 and a wide range of tourist facilities, including motels and hotels. It was born in 1883 as a tent town optimistically called Golden City. However, "City" was a rather presumptuous word to apply to the motley collection of log cabins and tents, two stores and a greater number of liquor outlets that catered to prospectors, miners and railroad workers. Liquor was the reason for Golden City's "wild and unsavory reputation" as one traveller wrote after he and his companions had pointedly detoured the community in 1884. In spite of the CPR's successful bid to have the sale of alcohol banned within 20 miles either side of the track, there was no restriction imposed on having it for private consumption. Large amounts of alcohol found its way in kegs along the Whiskey Trail from Sand Point south of the border. One traveller on the trail, stopping at a horse ranch, was so awed by the sight of packtrain hands sleeping off a night's carousing in Golden City that he declared "hog" ranch a better name — a name that stuck even though there were never any four-legged hogs in evidence.

Soon after the rails reached Golden City in November 1884, hotels sprang up to accommodate the travellers. One of the better known was the Queen's whose proprietor, J. C. Green, sallied forth to meet the train in a claw-hammer coat, top hat and white gloves. Startled passengers must have blinked hard and wondered if the Waldorf-Astoria had magically transported itself from New York City and landed in the wilds of the Canadian Rockies. However, their illusions were soon shattered by the primitive comforts of some of the hostelries. A story is told of one patron who asked where the washroom was. "Log out back," was the laconic reply.

He had not been there long when a bullet whizzed past his ear, followed by a terse request to move to the other end of the log. The hapless guest had unwittingly stood in the ladies section.

Golden's fandango days as a wild, tough town were not to last long. Once the railway was completed and the workers gone, the community smoothed its skirts and settled down to respectability. By 1888 traveller William Spotswood Green was able to write "we spent two safe and comfortable nights in Golden City."

(This is the end of the eastbound travel log from Revelstoke to Golden. Travellers heading west can follow the mileage backwards through Rogers Pass some 148 km (92 miles) to Revelstoke.)

Trip Notes